MW00913929

Learning How to Improve Vocabulary Instruction Through Teacher Study Groups

Learning How to Improve Vocabulary Instruction Through Teacher Study Groups

by

Joseph Dimino, Ph.D.

and

Mary Jo Taylor, Ed.D.

Instructional Research Group
Los Alamitos, California

Baltimore • London • Sydney

Paul H. Brookes Publishing Co.
Post Office Box 10624
Baltimore, Maryland 21285-0624
USA

www.brookespublishing.com

Copyright © 2009 by Paul H. Brookes Publishing Co.
All rights reserved.

"Paul H. Brookes Publishing Co." is a registered trademark
of Paul H. Brookes Publishing Co., Inc.

Typeset by Matrix Publishing Services, York, Pennsylvania.
Manufactured in the United States of America by
Sheridan Books, Inc., Chelsea, Michigan.

The definition on the following page is from *The American Heritage® Dictionary of the English Language, Fourth Edition,* copyright © 2000 by Houghton Mifflin Company. Updated in 2009. Published by Houghton Mifflin Company http://www.eref-trade.hmco.com. All rights reserved: 198 (somniloquy).

The definitions on the following pages are reproduced from "Collins Cobuild Advanced Learner's Dictionary" with the permission of HarperCollins Publishers Ltd. © HarperCollins Publishers Ltd. 2003. Updated from the Bank of English. Based on the Cobuild series, developed in collaboration with the University of Birmingham. Cobuild® and Bank of English® are registered trademarks of HarperCollins Publishers Ltd.: 45 (artist), 47 (vociferous, procrastinate), 50 (amazing), 51 (hungry, statue), 52 (splendid), 53 (taunt), 54 (disappointed), 55 (hoax, amiable), 70 (determined, procrastinate), 183 (vernacular), 187 (precious, wonderful, amazing), 188 (hungry, protect, statue), 189 (sensible, splendid, brave), 190 (crime, outspoken, taunt), 191 (oppose, disappointed, dread), 192 (hoax, conserve, amiable).

The definitions on the following pages are used by permission: From the *Merriam-Webster Online Dictionary* © 2009 by Merriam-Webster Incorporated (www.Merriam-Webster.com): 47 (procrastinate), 50 (precious, wonderful), 51 (protect), 52 (sensible, brave), 53 (crime, outspoken), 54 (oppose, dread), 55 (conserve), 187 (precious, wonderful), 188 (protect), 189 (sensible, brave), 190 (crime, outspoken), 191 (oppose, dread), 192 (conserve), 197 (canid), 198 (nescient).

The definition on the following page is used by permission from McKean, E. (Ed.). (2005). *The New Oxford American Dictionary* (2nd ed.). New York: Oxford University Press: 47 (vociferous).

Purchasers of *Learning How to Improve Vocabulary Instruction Through Teacher Study Groups* are granted permission to photocopy the blank forms on pages 26, 39, 58, 60, 79, 81, 103, 105–106, 115, 125–126, 156, 157, 158, 159, 167, and 177–178 for education purposes. None of the forms may be reproduced to generate revenue for any program or individual. Photocopies may only be made from an original book. *Unauthorized use beyond this privilege is prosecutable under federal law.* You will see the copyright protection notice at the bottom of each photocopiable page.

ISBN-13: 978-1-59857-054-0   ISBN-10: 1-59857-054-4

2012   2011   2010   2009
10   9   8   7   6   5   4   3   2   1

Contents

About the Authors

Joseph Dimino, Ph.D., Senior Research Associate, Instructional Research Group, 4281 Katella Avenue, Suite 205, Los Alamitos, California 90720

Since the early 1970s, Joseph A. Dimino has had experience as a general education teacher, a special education teacher, an administrator, a behavior consultant, and a researcher. He has extensive experience working with teachers, parents, administrators, and instructional assistants in the areas of instruction and early literacy, reading comprehension strategies, and classroom and behavior management in urban, suburban, and rural communities.

Dr. Dimino is a senior research associate at the Instructional Research Group in Los Alamitos, California, where he developed and conducted professional development as part of a national evaluation investigating the effectiveness of reading comprehension programs and is Co-principal Investigator for a study assessing the impact of Collaborative Strategic Reading on the comprehension and vocabulary skills of English language learners and English-speaking fifth graders. He is the professional development coordinator for a study investigating the impact of Teacher Study Groups on teaching practices and student vocabulary knowledge. He is also a panel member for the Response to Intervention (RTI) Reading Practice Guide and researcher for the RTI Mathematics Practice Guide, published by the National Center for Education Evaluation and Regional Assistance, Institute of Education Sciences, U.S. Department of Education (http://ies.ed.gov/ncee/wwc/publications/practiceguides). He served as one of the seven professional development staff members for the National Center on Student Progress Monitoring, a technical assistance and dissemination center funded by the Office of Special Education Programs within the U.S. Department of Education.

Dr. Dimino has co-authored books in reading comprehension and early reading intervention. He has published in numerous scholarly journals, including *Elementary School Journal, Reading Research Quarterly, The Journal of Learning Disabilities, Educational Leadership, Remedial and Special Education, Learning Disabilities Research and Practice, Learning Disability Quarterly, Exceptional Children, The Journal of Special Education*, and *Reading and Writing Quarterly*. He has delivered papers at numerous state, national, and international conferences, including the American Educational Research Association, the Society for the Scientific Study of Reading, the National Reading Conference, the International Reading Association, the Council for Exceptional Children, the Association for Supervision and Curriculum Development, the International Association of Applied Psychology, and the European Association for Research on Learning and Instruction. He consults nationally in the areas of early literacy and reading comprehension instruction.

Mary Jo Taylor, Ed.D., Senior Research Associate, Instructional Research Group, 4281 Katella Avenue, Suite 205, Los Alamitos, California 90720

Over the past 40 years, Dr. Taylor has served as a classroom and reading teacher, a building principal, a visiting professor, and a researcher. She was an assistant professor of Reading at John Carroll University in University Heights, Ohio, and a research associate for RMC Research Corporation in Arlington, Virginia. Currently, she is Senior Research Associate for the Instructional Research Group.

For 10 years, Dr. Taylor served as Title I coordinator and assumed leadership on numerous district-level committees, including Special Education, Curriculum Adoptions, Strategic Planning, and Middle School Reorganization. She was a hub leader for observers in the Reading First Impact Study and a professional development facilitator for Ohio's Reading First initiative. She has developed and conducted professional development as part of national evaluations investigating the effectiveness of reading comprehension programs and the impact of Collaborative Strategic Reading on the comprehension and vocabulary skills of English language learners and English-speaking fifth graders.

Dr. Taylor is currently a member of the national research team evaluating the implementation and effectiveness of Response to Intervention (RTI) strategies. Her work also expands into the area of mathematics, where she is developing and conducting training for a study evaluating the effectiveness of an RTI mathematics intervention.

Dr. Taylor graduated from Villa Maria College (now Gannon University) with a bachelor of arts degree in elementary education and a master's degree in elementary education, with an advanced degree as a reading specialist and school administrator. She completed her doctoral degree in the School of Leadership and Policy Studies at the University of Pittsburgh, with a focus on literacy. Dr. Taylor authored the paper *The Role of Literacy Specialists and the Ecological Conditions that Support Their Efficacy.* She also co-authored the paper *Facing the Future: A Status Report on Student Achievement in Ashtabula County, Report Prepared for Ashtabula Partnership for Continued Learning P-16 Councils.*

Dr. Taylor has delivered presentations at numerous, local, state, national, and international conferences, including the International Reading Association, the American Society for Quality, Phi Delta Kappa, and the Association for Supervision and Curriculum Development. She consults nationally in the areas of early literacy and reading comprehension instruction.

Acknowledgments

We recognize Lana Edwards-Santoro and Diane Haager for their assistance during the early stages of planning the Teacher Study Group (TSG) model. Kudos to Diane, Lana, Eve Puhalla, and Susan Shucker for serving as TSG facilitators. We thank the students, teachers, and administrators in Virginia, the Los Angeles Unified School District, and the School District of Philadelphia who participated in the investigation of the impact of TSGs on reading instruction. We extend a special thank you to Suellen Bowman, Elaine Livingston, and Cheryl Sheer for their contributions and thoughtful feedback and to Russell Gersten for his unwavering patience, support, and guidance. We gratefully acknowledge the funding provided by the U.S. Department of Education, Institute of Education Sciences, Grant R305M030052, which supported the development of the TSG model. The views expressed in this book are those of the authors and do not represent those of the funding agency.

Before You Begin

Improving Vocabulary Instruction Through Teacher Study Groups is based on a 2-year study conducted in three states where 86 teachers were randomly assigned to either the Teacher Study Group (TSG) or the control group condition. Positive effects on teacher practice and student achievement were found in the TSG condition. Results of research studies have shown that effective professional development programs allow participants to study topics in depth over an extended period of time. In this professional development module, major research-based concepts in vocabulary instruction are introduced and implemented over the course of a school year. The research on effective vocabulary instruction provides the foundation for the *content* of these sessions.

The sessions outlined in this book can be effectively conducted in groups (with or without a facilitator), in pairs, or by individuals. If the group is lead by a facilitator, we recommend someone who is an experienced literacy educator or someone who has participated in a group of this kind in the past. If the group is operating without a leader, the focus should be on collaboration, where everyone should feel comfortable participating. If you are working in pairs, we recommend alternating the leader role. If you are working individually, take advantage of the rich resources provided in this book to supplement your knowledge. No matter how you are learning, please use this book to its full potential!

Each member of the group should have his or her own copy of the book so that he or she can make notes and complete the activities. A few of the worksheets are meant to be photocopied so that you can practice the activities more than once. These worksheets are identified in the text and also by the copyright protection notice that appears at the bottom of these pages. No other section of the book may be photocopied (please refer to the photocopy notice on the copyright page of the book).

Many of the sessions reference the publisher's recommendations. In these instances, "the publisher" refers to the publisher of your core reading program, not the publisher of this book. The activities and worksheets will work with any reading program you are currently using.

We hope that you will take advantage of this book and the opportunity to learn from your colleagues and the research presented to improve your understanding of vocabulary instruction.

To our mothers, Cesina Marcantonio Dimino and Leah Licata

Introduction

Educators are inundated with invitations to attend 1-day professional development workshops. These invitations typically include testimonials from participants touting the benefits of a particular approach. However, the results of a study conducted by Garet, Porter, Desimone, Birman, and Yoon (2001) indicated that professional development is more likely to enhance teacher knowledge and skills if it provides an in-depth focus on academic subject matter (content), gives teachers opportunities for "hands-on" work (active learning), and is integrated into the daily life of the school (coherence). The content and processes of the Teacher Study Group (TSG) model are grounded on the premises of this solid research. This research covers areas that define ideal professional development for teachers. The following sections discuss how the TSG model addresses these points.

Content

The TSG model is intended to foster a deeper understanding of how scientifically based research in vocabulary is applied to classroom practice. The TSG sessions in this guide are patterned after a 2-year study conducted in three states in which 86 teachers were randomly assigned to either the TSG condition or the control group condition (Gersten, Dimino, Jayanthi, Kim, & Santoro, 2009). Positive effects on teacher practice and student achievement were found in the TSG condition. Results of research studies have shown that effective professional development programs allow participants to study topics in depth over an extended period of time (Gersten et al., 2009). In this professional development module, major research-based concepts in vocabulary instruction are introduced and implemented over the course of a school year. The research on effective vocabulary instruction provides the foundation for the content of these sessions.

Active Learning

The TSG format provides opportunities for teachers to actively learn together as they apply research-based concepts to classroom practice. Participants have the opportunity to share their knowledge and experiences in a setting that supports communication and collaboration. A key component of the TSG model is for par-

1

ticipants to help each other benefit from every session. Given the rich content in literacy instruction provided in each session, it is recommended that an educator with a strong literacy background serve as a facilitator to assist groups of teachers as they navigate through the research and apply it to their reading instruction.

Coherence

In professional development, coherence is perhaps one of the most critical attributes contributing to enduring teacher and school change. Birman, Desimone, Porter, and Garet (2000) define coherence as an integrated system of teacher learning. TSGs, an adaptation of the Japanese Lesson Study model (Fernandez & Chokshi, 2002; Watanabe, 2002) is one means of achieving coherence in professional development. It aligns with the school curriculum, focuses on the needs and learning goals of students, and can easily coincide with school- and district-wide change efforts. It helps teachers make sense of the priorities that are associated with school, district, and state initiatives.

The Structure and Purpose of the Teacher Study Group Sessions

Learning How to Improve Vocabulary Instruction Through Teacher Study Groups follows a specific format to enhance learning. The following sections describe this overall structure and the purpose of each element.

Structure

A five-phase process for learning is repeated during each of the sessions: 1) Debrief, 2) Discuss the Focus Research Concept, 3) Compare Research with Practice, 4) Plan Collaboratively, and 5) Assignment. Participants begin by debriefing the lesson they collaboratively planned in the previous session. Participants describe the lesson they taught, report on any changes or adjustments they made while teaching the lesson, and discuss how students responded. During Discuss the Focus Research Concept portion, a new research concept is presented. Participants review, reflect on, and discuss the concept before proceeding to the Compare Research with Practice segment, where they compare the instructional design of their core reading program with the focus research concept. Then, participants incorporate the research into the lesson they collaboratively plan. At the end of each session, participants are given an assignment that they will need to complete before their next meeting. This usually involves implementing the lesson they developed during the session.

Purpose

The purpose of this book is to provide the group with a specific "game plan" for the five-phase, recursive process. For each session, the reader is provided with a focus research concept, cumulative review, goals, an overview, and instructions for completing the five phases (Debrief, Discuss the Focus Research Concept, Compare

Research with Practice, Plan Collaboratively, and Assignment). Each segment of the TSG sessions is described next.

Focus Research Concept

The focus research concept studied in the session is identified. To ensure that participants have an opportunity to discuss and apply the concept to classroom practice, only one focus research concept is highlighted during the Compare Research with Practice and Plan Collaboratively portions of the session.

Cumulative Review

Cumulative review is incorporated into selected sessions. Cumulative reviews help participants practice, retain, and routinely implement the research concepts that they have learned in previous sessions.

Session Goals

Session goals give the TSG participants a clear and concise idea of the nature of the session by listing the goals they should achieve by the end of the session.

Overview of the Session

The purpose of the overview is to provide a short synopsis of the research concept that will be introduced, identify concepts that will be discussed, and describe activities participants will complete during the session.

Debrief

Debriefing is the first phase of the five-phase recursive process. In this section, questions are provided to help participants discuss their implementation of the lesson they planned collaboratively during the previous session.

Discuss the Focus Research Concept

During the TSG sessions, participants read a worksheet describing the focus research concept that will be highlighted during the session. Participants are asked to read it and complete the study guide that is provided. The study guide is used to help participants focus their attention on the salient features of the reading. It is an important tool to help participants process and retain the information. During this portion of the session, we recommend that the participants discuss responses to the study guide questions and use the activities provided to underscore the most critical aspects of the focus research concept.

Compare Research with Practice

Participants review the publisher's recommendations for teaching a selection from their core reading program. Their charge is to determine how these recommendations did or did not exemplify the tenets of the focus research concept they discussed in the Discuss the Focus Research Concept segment of the session. To that end, this portion of the session contains three segments: Preview the Activity, Practice the Activity, and Discuss the Activity. For those participants who use a reading program that does not include a teacher's edition, it will be necessary to compare the contents of their lesson plan with the focus research concept.

- *Preview the Activity:* Participants are given an explanation of the procedures for comparing the instructional design of the core reading program with the focus research concept.

- *Practice the Activity:* In a large group, in a small group, or in pairs, the participants follow the step-by-step procedure provided in the task analysis sheet to compare how the lesson design in the core reading program aligns with the focus research concept.

- *Discuss the Activity:* The participants are provided with questions to promote discussion regarding the nature and degree of research-based evidence found in their core reading program.

Plan Collaboratively

Based on the their analysis from the Compare Research with Practice segment of the session, participants work as a whole group, in small groups, or in pairs to integrate the focus research concept into their current reading program. They do this by designing lessons that infuse the key focus research concept that is not evident in the teacher's edition. Task Analysis worksheets and related worksheets are provided to guide participants in these activities.

Assignment

This section of the session lists the assignment participants must complete before the next TSG session. Typically, participants are asked to teach the lesson they developed.

Recommendations for Time Allotment

We recommend that TSG sessions convene two times per month for 75–90 minutes. If this is not possible, it may be necessary to conduct the sessions weekly for 30–45 minutes. It is not possible to complete all phases of the session appropriately in this abbreviated time period. Therefore, we recommend addressing the Debrief and Discuss the Focus Research Concept phases in one session and the remaining phases in a follow-up session. Generally, the activities in the Discuss the Focus Research Concept phase are listed in priority order. Start with the first activity and complete as many activities as possible within the suggested time allotment. Conversely, none of the activities in the Compare Research with Practice and Plan Collaboratively phases should be omitted. Assignments should not be eliminated, as they provide the foundation for the next session. The following table lists the phases of the TSG session and time recommendations for 75–90 minute sessions.

Phase	Time allotment
Debrief	10 minutes
Discuss the Focus Research Concept	15–20 minutes
Compare Research with Practice	20–25 minutes
Plan Collaboratively	30–35 minutes

References

Birman, B.F., Desimone, L., Porter, A.C., & Garet, M.S. (2000). Designing professional development that works. *Educational Leadership, 57*, 28–33.

Fernandez, C., & Chokshi, S. (2002). A practical guide to translating lesson study for a U.S. setting. *Phi Delta Kappan, 64*(2), 128–134.

Garet, M.S., Porter, A.C., Desimone, L., & Yoon, K.S. (2001). What makes professional development effective? Results from a national sample of teachers. *American Educational Research Journal, 38*, 915–945.

Gersten, R., Dimino, J., Jayanthi, M., Kim, J., & Santoro, L. (2009). *An investigation of the impact of the Teacher Study Groups as a means to enhance the quality of reading comprehension and vocabulary instruction for first graders in Reading First schools: Technical Report.* Los Alamitos, CA: Instructional Research Group. (http://www.inresg.org)

Watanabe, T. (2002). Learning from Japanese lesson study. *Educational Leadership, 59*(6), 36–39.

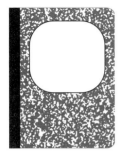

Teacher Study Groups

FOCUS RESEARCH CONCEPT

- Effective, Research-Based Professional Development and the TSG Model

SESSION GOALS

1. Review the research-based criteria established for high-quality professional development.
2. Become acquainted with the TSG professional development model.
3. Determine meeting schedules and the protocol for upcoming sessions.

TSGs

ORIENTATION

Overview of the Session

The TSG professional development model is intended to foster a deeper understanding of how scientifically based research in vocabulary is applied to classroom practice. This study group format provides opportunities for you to study and learn together as you apply research-based concepts to classroom practice. You will have the opportunity to share your knowledge and experiences in a setting that supports communication and collaboration. A key component of the TSG model is for participants to help each other benefit from every session. In this professional development program, major research concepts in vocabulary instruction are introduced and implemented over the course of a school year. The content of the professional development sessions is based on current literature in effective vocabulary instruction.

This program features two of the four aspects of a comprehensive approach to vocabulary instruction: teaching individual words and word consciousness. It was written based on a 2-year randomized control trial that we conducted to determine the effects of TSG on pedagogy and student achievement in vocabulary and comprehension (Gersten, Dimino, Jayanthi, Kim, & Santoro, 2009). Positive effects on teacher practice and student achievement were found in the TSG condition. We purposely focused our research on professional development aimed at improving educators' ability to teach vocabulary directly and explicitly. We recognize that wide reading and word learning strategies are important aspects of vocabulary instruction. These aspects were not investigated in our research. Therefore, they are not addressed in this program.

A five-phase process is repeated during each of the sessions. This recursive process includes the following components: 1) Debrief, 2) Discuss the Focus Research Concept, 3) Compare Research with Practice, 4) Plan Collaboratively, and 5) Assignment. You will begin by debriefing the lesson you collaboratively planned in the previous session. First, you and other group members will describe the lessons you taught, discuss how students responded, and indicate any changes or adjustments you made while teaching the lesson. A new research concept is presented during the Discuss the Focus Research Concept portion of the session. You will review, reflect on, and discuss the focus research concept before proceeding to the Compare Research with Practice portion of the session. In this segment of the session, you will compare the instructional design of your core reading program with the focus research concept. Next, you will incorporate the focus research concept into a lesson you have collaboratively planned. Finally, you will be given an assignment to complete before the next session. Typically, you will be asked to implement the lesson you developed during the session.

Debrief

Begin by sharing prior professional development experiences with the group. Tell which types of professional development experiences helped you transfer your new learning to changes in classroom practice and which experiences did not. Discuss possible reasons for these differences. Using chart paper, an overhead transparency, or a white board, make two columns labeled *Effective* and *Not Effective*. As these experiences are shared, list the *Effective* and *Not Effective* factors in their respective columns.

Discuss the Focus Research Concept

1. The TSG sessions are organized around research-based concepts in vocabulary instruction. Use Worksheet A: Scope and Sequence of Vocabulary Concepts: Teacher Study Groups to review the research-based concepts that will be addressed in each session. During this portion of the session, you will have the opportunity to discuss the interpretations and implications of the research concepts and apply them to your classroom practice.

2. TSGs provide a model for professional development that replicates the processes and procedures used with the teachers in the 2-year study. Use Worksheet B: Recursive Process of the Teacher Study Group Sessions to review the recursive model that will be used during each session. The sessions begin by debriefing the lesson you collaboratively planned in the previous session. This includes a discussion of how the lesson went, how students responded, and which changes or adjustments you made while teaching the lesson. A new research concept is then presented. You will be asked to review, reflect on, and discuss the research concept before comparing how it aligns with your core reading program. You will incorporate the focus research concept into the lesson you plan collaboratively.

3. Because you did not have a lesson to debrief, this session will start with a discussion of your previous professional development experiences. In subsequent sessions, you will be discussing the lessons you planned collaboratively and implemented with your students.

4. For today's review of the focus research concept, read the descriptions of the characteristics of high-quality professional development listed in the left column of Worksheet C: Comparing the Characteristics of Effective, Research-Based Professional Development (Dole, 2003; Elmore, 2002; Garet, Porter, Desimone, Birman, & Yoon, 2001; Gusky, 2003).

5. After you have reviewed the characteristics of high-quality professional development, discuss the following questions:

    a. According to research, what are the five key characteristics of effective professional development?

    b. Using Worksheet C: Comparing the Characteristics of Effective, Research-Based Professional Development, discuss how the aspects of the TSG model correspond with the key characteristics of research-based effective professional development.

Compare Research with Practice

1. The Compare Research with Practice segment of each session allows you to determine the gaps between the research and the instructional design of your core reading program. During the Compare Research with Practice portion of the session, you will be examining the alignment between the research you read and the core reading program.

2. Today you will use Worksheet C: Comparing the Characteristics of Effective, Research-Based Professional Development to compare the characteristics of effective research-based professional development with the way professional development is normally conducted in your district.

3. Think of a professional development program you have attended recently. Compare the key characteristics of that professional development program with the characteristics of effective, research-based professional development by completing the last column in the Worksheet C: Comparing the Characteristics of Effective, Research-Based Professional Development.

4. Share your analysis.

Plan Collaboratively

1. The Plan Collaboratively segment of the sessions allows you to address the gaps between the focus research concept and the instructional design of your core reading program. Using the information you gathered in the Compare Research with Practice segment of the session, you will incorporate the focus research concept (e.g., Developing Student Friendly Definitions) into a lesson that you will deliver to your students before the next session.

2. For this session's Plan Collaboratively segment, discuss the logistics and schedule for the sessions (e.g., "We will meet twice monthly for 10 weeks, every other Thursday in the library").

3. Discuss ground rules for working as a group. Write them on chart paper, a whiteboard, or an overhead transparency. You may prepare a handout of the ground rules that will be distributed during the Debrief portion of Session 1. Here are some recommendations for ground rules that will help your study group function effectively and efficiently:

   • Attend all sessions.

   • Come prepared for each session by teaching the lesson you planned during the previous session.

   • Be respectful and courteous to each other.

   • Everyone should participate.

   • If you miss a session, determine what you will need to do to be ready for the next session.

Assignment

1. An assignment will be given at the end of most sessions and will need to be completed before the next session. The assignment usually includes implementing the lesson that you developed during the Collaborative Planning portion of the session.

2. There is no assignment for the next session.

References

Dole, J.A. (2003). Professional development in reading comprehension instruction. In A.P. Sweet & C.E. Snow (Eds.), *Rethinking reading comprehension* (pp. 176–191). New York: The Guilford Press.

Elmore, R.F. (2002). *Bridging the gap between standards and achievement: The imperative for professional development in education.* Washington, DC: Albert Shanker Institute.

Garet, M.S., Porter, A., Desimone, L., Birman, B.F., & Yoon, K.W. (2001). What makes professional development effective? Results from a national sample of teachers. *American Educational Research Journal, 38,* 915–945.

Gersten, R., Dimino, J., Jayanthi, M., Kim, J., & Santoro, L. (2009). *An investigation of the impact of the Teacher Study Groups as a means to enhance the quality of reading comprehension and vocabulary instruction for first graders in Reading First schools: Technical Report.* Los Alamitos, CA: Instructional Research Group. (http://www.inresg.org)

Gusky, T. (2003). What makes professional development effective? *Phi Delta Kappan, 84,* 748–750.

Scope and Sequence of Vocabulary Concepts

Teacher Study Groups

Session 1 Words in Context

Session 2 Selecting Words

Session 3 Student Friendly Definitions

Session 4 Examples, Nonexamples, and Concrete Representations

Session 5 Activities to Promote Word Learning

Session 6 Cumulative Review I

Session 7 Using Context to Determine Word Meanings

Session 8 Reviewing and Extending Word Learning

Session 9 Cumulative Review II

Recursive Process of the Teacher Study Group Sessions

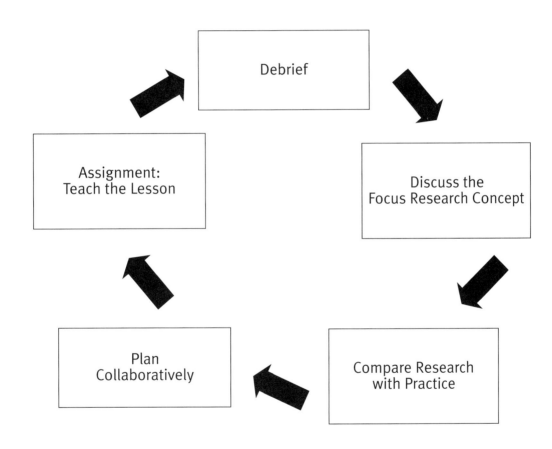

Debrief

Assignment:
Teach the Lesson

Discuss the
Focus Research Concept

Plan
Collaboratively

Compare Research
with Practice

Comparing the Characteristics of Effective, Research-Based Professional Development

Sources: Dole, 2003; Elmore, 2002; Garet, Porter, Desimone, Birman, & Yoon, 2001; Gusky, 2003

Characteristics of high-quality professional development	Teacher study group (TSG)	Current professional development programs

1. Increase teacher knowledge
  a. Increases teachers' subject matter knowledge (e. g., teachers understand the critical features of effective vocabulary instruction)
  b. Leads to teachers' increased pedagogical knowledge (e.g., teachers know how to develop and deliver a lesson that incorporates the critical features of effective vocabulary instruction)
	1. Increase teacher knowledge
	  Participants in the study were administered a teacher knowledge test. In addition, their instructional practices were measured by classroom observations of vocabulary instruction. Vocabulary knowledge and instructional practices of teachers in the TSG condition were significantly better than those of the comparison teachers.	

2. Sufficient duration and intensity
  a. Continues over an extended time span with follow-up sessions over the course of the year
  b. Studies content and pedagogical topics in depth (e.g., several sessions are spent on the same topic)
	2. Sufficient duration and intensity
	  Participants met two times per month for 75 minutes over 8 months. Topics from previous sessions were reviewed and reinforced frequently over the course of the program.	

3. Collective participation a. Includes content teachers working together (e.g., reading, social studies, math) b. Involves teachers working in grade-level teams (e.g., second-grade team or K–2 team) c. Utilizes study groups; involves collaborative planning and problem solving	3. Collective participation Each session included teachers working in grade-level teams to debrief on previously taught lessons, discuss the research-based concepts presented, align these concepts with their core program, and plan a lesson by collaboratively applying new research to classroom practice.	
4. Coherence a. Aligns with school curriculum and focuses on the needs of students and their learning goals b. Coincides with school- and district-wide change efforts	4. Coherence The TSG was aligned with the professional development goals of Reading First. It incorporated activities that compared instruction in the core reading program with research-based practices.	
5. Active learning a. Provides teachers with a model, opportunities to practice new strategies, and feedback on their implementation b. Includes coaching and/or mentoring to help participants apply concepts in their classrooms c. Examines student work	5. Active learning TSG sessions were conducted at the school site by a knowledgeable facilitator. TSG sessions provided teachers with a model of the characteristics of effective vocabulary instruction and an opportunity to teach and debrief lessons they planned collaboratively.	

REFERENCES

Dole, J.A. (2003). Professional development in reading comprehension instruction. In A.P. Sweet & C.E. Snow (Eds.), *Rethinking reading comprehension* (pp. 176–191). New York: The Guilford Press.

Elmore, R.F. (2002). *Bridging the gap between standards and achievement: The imperative for professional development in education*. Washington, DC: Albert Shanker Institute.

Garet, M.S., Porter, A., Desimone, L., Birman, B.F., & Yoon, K.W. (2001). What makes professional development effective? Results from a national sample of teachers. *American Educational Research Journal, 38*, 915–945.

Gusky, T. (2003). What makes professional development effective? *Phi Delta Kappan, 84*, 748–750.

VOCABULARY SESSION

Words in Context

FOCUS RESEARCH CONCEPT

- Categories of Natural Context: Misdirective, Nondirective, Directive, and General

SESSION GOALS

1. Understand and recognize the four categories of natural context.
2. Learn the process for determining which words are appropriate for teaching students prior to reading a selection.
3. Select words to teach prior to students reading a selection in the core reading program.

Overview of the Session

This session addresses two important concepts you need to consider before introducing vocabulary. The first is to understand and be able to recognize the four categories of natural context in which words occur in connected text. Second, you need to learn how to determine which words are appropriate to teach prior to reading the selection and which words can be taught using context.

In the first part of the session, debrief on the key aspects of the TSG model from the previous session followed by a review of Worksheet 1B: Words in Context. Next, review the vocabulary words in the teacher's edition that the publisher recommends teaching students before they read the selection. Place each of the recommended vocabulary words into the appropriate context category (i.e., misdirective, nondirective, directive, and general). Then determine if you agree or disagree with the publisher's recommendation that the vocabulary word should be taught before the selection is read. Finally, apply these same procedures to the next selection in your core reading program.

Debrief

A recursive format will be used in each of the TSG sessions. Discuss the following questions.

- What ground rules were established in the previous session?

- What are some of the key aspects of the TSG model?

- How do these correspond to the characteristics of high-quality professional development?

- How will the recursive format of the TSG affect your practice? Your students?

- To what extent will this professional development model enhance your curriculum?

Discuss the Focus Research Concept

1. Notice the topic of this session, Words in Context.

2. Using Worksheet 1A: Categories of Natural Context, note the four categories of natural context developed by Beck and her colleagues (Beck, McKeown, & McCaslin, 1983; Beck, McKeown, & Kucan, 2002). In order to determine the words that should be taught before students read a selection, you must first determine whether the context in which the words appear will help or hinder students' ability to determine a word's meaning.

3. Read more about words in their natural contexts in Worksheet 1B: Words in Context.

4. Discuss the four categories of natural context (i.e., misdirective, nondirective, directive, and general). Use the descriptions and examples in Worksheet 1B: Words in Context to understand the differences in the categories. Discuss why

words in the misdirective and nondirective contexts are chosen most often for teaching before students read a selection.

5. For additional practice on the four categories of natural context, complete the exercises in Worksheet 1C: Study Guide: Words in Context.

6. Use the answer key to check your answers to Worksheet 1C: Study Guide: Words in Context (see the appendix at the end of the book).

Compare Research with Practice

Preview the Activity

1. You will be reviewing the vocabulary words in the teacher's edition that the publisher recommends teaching students before they read the selection. The purpose of this activity will be to place each of the recommended words in the appropriate context category (i.e., misdirective, nondirective, directive, and general) and to determine if you agree or disagree with the publisher's recommendation. Typically, words in the nondirective and misdirective categories should be explicitly taught, whereas words in general and directive contexts either do not need to be taught or need only a cursory explanation and/or minor clarification.

2. You will choose a selection you will be teaching within the next week and identify a word from a selection that the publisher has chosen for instruction.

3. You will read the sentence with the target word in it and the set of sentences surrounding it (i.e., the sentences before and after) and identify the category of natural context in which the target word belongs.

4. Then you will agree or disagree that the word should be taught before students read the selection.

5. You will repeat this process with at least two more words.

Practice the Activity

1. Turn to Worksheet 1D: Task Analysis: Categories of Natural Context and Worksheet 1E: Categories of Natural Context Table. Use the task analysis to guide you through the activity.

2. Continue this activity until all of the recommended vocabulary words in the selection have been analyzed.

Discuss the Activity

Discuss the following questions:

a. In which category did most of the publisher's recommendations belong?

b. Did you mostly agree or disagree with the words the publisher recommends teaching students before they read the selection? Explain.

Plan Collaboratively

1. Make a few copies of Worksheet 1E: Categories of Natural Context Table.

2. Apply the procedures from Compare Research with Practice: Practice the Activity to the next selection in the core reading program. Use Worksheet 1D: Task Analysis: Categories of Natural Context to guide you through the activity.

Assignment

There is no assignment for the next session.

WORKSHEET 1A

Categories of Natural Context

1

1. Misdirective: The context leads the reader toward the incorrect meaning of the word.

2. Nondirective: The context does not assist the reader in determining the meaning of the target word.

3. Directive: There is enough information to lead students to the correct meaning of the word, or the word is explicitly defined and/or explained in the text.

4. General: The context provides readers with adequate information to give them a general idea of the word's meaning.

Words in Context

The first step in designing effective vocabulary lessons is to understand and distinguish the variety of ways words appear in context. It is impossible to preteach all of the difficult words in a selection. Identifying the context in which words appear is a factor to consider when determining whether a word should be taught before students read connected text. It is important to recognize whether the context will help or hinder students in determining a word's meaning.

Beck and her colleagues (1983, 2002) analyzed the natural context for words students were expected to learn from context. As a result of their extensive analysis, they developed a continuum that categorizes the degree to which the context supports the reader in deriving the word's meaning. The four categories of natural context are identified as misdirective, nondirective, directive, and general.

Misdirective contexts lead the reader toward an incorrect meaning for the word. Consider the following example for the word *elated*: "Winners of the pretrial race were preparing for the final contest. As Roberta watched her husband take his starting position, her heart began to beat violently under her sweatshirt. She knew he had a good chance to win this one, and if he lost she would be elated."

Most readers would predict that *elated* means disappointed. The author indicated that this was an important race for Roberta's husband to win. The description of Roberta's physical reaction would lead the reader to deduce that she would be disappointed if her husband lost the race; however, when they read the next paragraph they will discover that Roberta is tired of all of the travel, drama, and potential danger surrounding the racing world. She is hoping that her husband will lose the race and stop competing so he can stay home with his family. In this example, the misdirective context in which the word is used leads the reader to infer the incorrect meaning.

Nondirective contexts do not contain enough information to help the reader determine the meaning of the target word, as in *frail* in the following example: "Jamie was excited to be visiting his grandparents after so many years. He scanned the crowd waiting in the airport lounge until he recognized the worn brown bomber jacket he remembered so well from his childhood walks in the woods. It was his grandfather's favorite memento from his flying days. As he raced to embrace him, Jamie noticed the woman standing by his side. Could this frail woman be his grandmother?"

In this passage, it is not possible to determine the exact meaning of the word *frail*. It could mean almost anything that the speaker might find surprising: lovely, old, or even bald. The nondirective context does not contain sufficient clues to help the reader formulate a definition.

Directive contexts contain enough information to lead students to the correct meaning of the word. This category includes words that are explicitly defined or explained in the text. *Amendment* is explicitly explained in this example: "After more than 200 years, the

---

United States Constitution continues to work. Our Founding Fathers made sure that it could be changed to meet the needs of our country by allowing a system for adding amendments. Amendments are sections added to a law or a rule to change it. In more than 200 years, only 27 amendments, or additions, have been made to our Constitution."

In this example of directive context, the definition and purpose of *amendment* are clearly explained. The context does not require readers to integrate their background knowledge with the text to attempt to determine the word's meaning nor does the context mislead the reader into formulating an incorrect definition.

General contexts provide the reader with adequate information to give a general idea of the word's meaning. (Determining the definition of words in general contexts is the focus of Session 7.) Consider the following example with the word *winced*: "The political candidate, filled with confidence and energy, came to the podium. He answered questions without saying anything controversial and seemed to be pleasing the crowd. The last question of the press conference included new information about the corruption of a former employee. His campaign manager's face tightened as he winced in reaction to the unscripted answer of his candidate."

In this example, the meaning of *winced* is not explicitly stated. There is information (e.g., his face tightened) in the passage to convey the idea that *winced* seems to have something to do with a facial expression that was a negative reaction to the compromising question about corruption.

REFERENCES

Beck, I.L., McKeown, M.G., & McCaslin, E.S. (1983). Vocabulary development: All contexts are not created equal. *The Elementary School Journal, 83,* 177–181.

Beck, I.L., McKewon, M.G., & Kucan, L. (2002). *Bringing words to life: Robust vocabulary instruction.* New York: The Guilford Press.

Study Guide

WORKSHEET 1C

Words in Context

1

Directions: Determine the context category (i.e., misdirective, nondirective, directive, or general) of the bolded words in each of the following paragraphs.

1. When they visited the desert retreat, Judy and her mother enjoyed swimming, playing tennis, and having spa treatments in the cactus gardens. Because of the effects of the **sere** weather, they had moisturizing facials every day. Even so, they were happy to return to their beachfront home.

   Context Category: _____

2. We were having our annual staff luncheon at the local Italian restaurant, Giuseppe's Trattoria. The food was excellent and our large group was having a wonderful time. Gaetano, the owner, was **equanimous** when several of his relatives dropped in unexpectedly.

   Context Category: _____

3. There are many similarities and differences between mammals and birds. The bone structure of a bird's wing bears an uncanny resemblance to the bone structure of the human arm. The **hallux,** or big toe, of most mammals aligns with the other toes. In birds, the comparable digit usually turns backward.

   Context Category: _____

4. A group of residents had gathered in the coffeehouse to visit and listen to the weekly literary readings and interpretations by a local college professor known for his eloquent speaking style. The audience was impressed by the speaker's use of **vernacular** language when reading his newest poetry.

   Context Category: _____

Task Analysis

Categories of Natural Context

Directions: Choose a selection in the core reading program. Use the following steps to determine the category of natural context for each word the publisher recommends teaching students before they read the selection. Determine if you agree or disagree with the publisher's recommendation.

1. Enter the recommended words in the first column on Worksheet 1E: Categories of Natural Context Table.

2. Determine the category of natural context in which each word fits (i.e., misdirective and nondirective, directive, general). Designate the category by placing a checkmark in either the second, third, or fourth column. Typically, words in the nondirective and misdirective categories should be explicitly taught; words in general and directive contexts either do not need to be taught or need a cursory explanation and/or clarification.

3. Decide whether you agree or disagree with the publisher's recommendation that the word should be explicitly taught. Indicate your decision by placing a checkmark in either the Agree or the Disagree column.

4. If there are fewer than five recommended words, use words from more than one selection until you have at least five words. In this case, use another copy of Worksheet 1E.

5. Review the distribution of words in the categories of natural context. Be ready to discuss the following questions:

   a. In which category of natural context did most of the publisher's recommendations belong?

   b. Did you mostly agree or disagree with the words the publisher recommends teaching students before they read the selection?

1

Categories of Natural Context Table

Selection: _____

Recommended vocabulary	Category of natural context			Should be taught?	
	Nondirective or Misdirective	Directive	General	Agree	Disagree

Learning How to Improve Vocabulary Instruction Through Teacher Study Groups by Joseph Dimino & Mary Jo Taylor
Copyright © 2009 by Paul H. Brookes Publishing Co., Inc. All rights reserved.

Selecting Words

FOCUS RESEARCH CONCEPT

• Selecting Words to Teach

CUMULATIVE REVIEW

• Categories of Natural Context: Misdirective, Nondirective, Directive, and General

SESSION GOALS

1. Understand the criteria for selecting words to teach.
2. Categorize words into three tiers.
3. Choose words in the core program that require brief instruction and more elaborate instruction.

2

Overview of the Session

Some of the key principles guiding teachers in selecting words to teach are highlighted in this session. Topics include the criteria for selecting words and what to do if there are not enough words in a selection. The session will begin with a debriefing of the previous session on distinguishing categories of natural context followed by a review of Worksheet 2A: Selecting Words to Teach. You will then follow a series of steps that outline how to choose the most critical words to teach in a selection. The purpose of this activity is to help you to identify the text factors, student factors, and the tier level of words before making decisions. It also helps you to distinguish those words needing brief instruction from those that will require more elaborate instruction. Finally, you will apply the procedures to at least one selection in your core reading program.

Debrief

Review the four categories of natural context: misdirective, nondirective, directive, and general. During the collaborative planning portion of the last session, you reviewed the vocabulary words the publisher recommended teaching students before they read the selection. Your task was to place each of the recommended vocabulary words in the appropriate context category and to determine if you agree or disagree with the publisher's recommendations.

Discuss the category in which most of the words belong and explain why you agree or disagree with the publisher's recommended words. Reflect on the following questions.

- In which category of natural context did most of the publisher's recommendations belong?

- Did you mostly agree or disagree with the words the publisher recommends teaching before reading the selection?

- Discuss the rationale for your decisions.

Discuss the Focus Research Concept

1. This session will focus on key principles for selecting words to teach.

2. Read Worksheet 2A: Selecting Words to Teach. As you read the selection, think about the first question in Worksheet 2B: Study Guide: Selecting Words to Teach. After reading, write your response in the study guide.

3. Share your responses to Question 1 of Worksheet 2B: Study Guide: Selecting Words to Teach.

4. Complete a semantic map to summarize the factors teachers should consider when selecting words to teach. There are two options for conducting this activity:

    a. You will complete Worksheet 2C: Semantic Map: Selecting Words to Teach with a partner or in a small group. (See the appendix at the end of the book for the answer key for Worksheet 2B: Study Guide: Selecting Words to Teach.) Discuss the statements you recorded under each category.

b. A facilitator could lead your group through the activity by eliciting your responses to Worksheet 2C: Semantic Map: Selecting Words to Teach. (See the appendix at the end of the book for the answer key to Worksheet 2C: Semantic Map: Selecting Words to Teach.) The facilitator will record your statements as you respond.

5. Work in pairs to complete Question 2 of Worksheet 2B: Study Guide: Selecting Words to Teach.

6. After you have completed sorting words independently, discuss the criteria you used for placing words into tiers by sharing your responses to Question 2 of Worksheet 2B: Study Guide: Selecting Words to Teach. Be ready to justify your answers. (See the appendix at the end of the book for the answer key to Worksheet 2B: Study Guide: Selecting Words to Teach).

Compare Research with Practice

Preview the Activity

1. The purpose of this exercise is to determine 1) if there is agreement with the publisher regarding which words should be taught before reading; and 2) of those words, which words will require brief instruction and which require more elaborate instruction. You will be choosing a selection in the core reading program that you will be teaching before the next session. You will read the selection and review each recommended vocabulary word. You will be provided with a task analysis to assist you in completing the activity.

2. The first step in selecting words to teach is to determine if they should be placed in a word bank (Worksheet 2D: Selecting Words to Teach Table). A word is put in the word bank if it meets the following criteria: 1) it is in a misdirective/nondirective context, 2) it is critical for understanding the selection, 3) students have had limited knowledge of and exposure to the word, and 4) it is important for future learning.

3. Before you begin, look at Worksheet 2E: Cooperative Parenting. As you read the selection, focus on the words *vociferous* and *enormous*. The publisher recommends that you teach these words before students read the selection.

4. In this passage, the word *vociferous* belongs in the directive category because it is explicitly explained in the text. The word *vociferous* belongs in the directive category. Words that belong in the directive and general category typically will not need to be explicitly taught. The meanings of these words can be determined by context or are defined in the text.

5. Next, analyze the word *enormous*. *Enormous* belongs in the nondirective category as the context does not help the reader determine the meaning of the word. Therefore, you would keep the word *enormous* in mind for possible placement in the word bank.

6. The next step in deciding whether a word should be placed in the word bank is to determine if knowing its meaning is critical for understanding the selection. The word *enormous* is conceptually central to understanding the selection. The reader must understand that the penguins have to stand together in a large group to stay warm in order to successfully complete the incubation process. Keep *enormous* in mind as a possible word to include in the word bank.

7. Once you have determined that *enormous* is conceptually central to understanding the passage, there are other important factors you will need to consider to determine whether a word should be taught. They are: 1) the students' knowledge of and exposure to the word; and, 2) the importance of the word for future learning. You would ask yourself two questions:

   a. Has the student had sufficient previous experience with or exposure to the word *enormous*?

   b. Will the word *enormous* be important for the student to know 5 years from now?

   The word *enormous* is in a third-grade passage. Typically, many third graders have had little or no experience with or exposure to this word. This is a word that a mature language learner would use frequently across a variety of subject areas, so it would be considered important for a student to know 5 years from now. Based on these criteria, the word *enormous* should be placed in the word bank. A word is placed in the word bank only if a student has not had sufficient previous experience with a word and if that word will be important 5 years from now.

8. You will follow the same procedure for the remaining recommended words to determine which of the words belong in the word bank.

9. The next step is to determine whether each word placed in the word bank is a Tier 1, Tier 2, or Tier 3 word. You will enter each word in the appropriate column.

10. The word *enormous* is a Tier 2 word and should be placed in the Tier 2 column on Worksheet 2D: Selecting Words to Teach Table.

11. Next, you will circle the Tier 2 words that are most necessary for comprehending the selection. You will use your best judgment when making these decisions. Consider important factors such as the students' socioeconomic status (SES), prior knowledge, and English language proficiency.

12. You will also circle Tier 1 and Tier 3 words that are critical for comprehending the selection. Take into consideration the important factors previously discussed.

13. The final step is to decide which of the circled words need only brief instruction and which need more elaborate instruction. Use your best judgment to

make these decisions. Elaborate instruction is necessary for teaching the word *enormous*. Both elaborate and brief instruction include a student friendly definition, examples, nonexamples, and concrete representations. Only words requiring elaborate instruction include activities to promote word learning. The word *enormous* should be written in the Elaborate Instruction column.

Practice the Activity

1. You will be working with a selection to determine if there is agreement with the publisher regarding which words should be taught before reading and, of those words, which will require brief instruction and which will require more elaborate instruction.

2. Make a copy of Worksheet 2D: Selecting Words to Teach Table.

3. Choose a selection in the core reading program. Review the words the publisher recommends teaching students before they read the selection.

4. Read the selection. Follow the steps below for each recommended word to determine if it requires brief instruction or elaborate instruction. Teach no more than 10 words per selection.

Step 1   Does the word belong in the misdirective or nondirective category? If so, proceed to Step 2. This word may be a candidate for the word bank. If not, proceed to the next word. Descriptions of the natural context categories are as follows:

- Misdirective: The context leads the reader toward the incorrect meaning of the word.

- Nondirective: The context does not assist the reader in determining the meaning of the target word.

- Directive: There is enough information to lead the reader to the correct meaning of the word, or the word is explicitly defined or explained in the text.

- General: The context provides the reader with adequate information to give a general idea of the word's meaning.

Step 2   Is the word critical (i.e., conceptually central) for understanding the selection? If so, proceed to Step 3. If not, proceed to the next word.

Step 3   Next, consider the student factors.

a. Ask yourself if the students had sufficient previous experience with or exposure to the word.

b. Ask yourself if the word will be important for students to know 5 years from now.

c. Write the word in the word bank if you decided that students have not had sufficient previous experience with or exposure to the word and it will be important for them to know 5 years from now. Repeat these steps for the remaining words before proceeding to Step 4.

Step 4   Determine whether each word in the word bank is a Tier 1, Tier 2, or Tier 3 word. Enter each word in the appropriate column. Descriptions of the tiers are as follows:

- Tier 1 are the most basic words (e.g., *desk*, *run*, *house*). Students rarely need to be taught these words.

- Tier 2 are high frequency words for mature language users and are found across a variety of subject areas (e.g., *adequate*, *enormous*, *vociferous*, *satisfactory*).

- Tier 3 words are used infrequently and are often limited to a specific subject area (e.g., *chlorophyll*, *archipelago*, *diode*, *ventricle*).

Step 5   Circle the Tier 2 words that are most necessary for comprehending the selection. Again, consider such factors as the importance of the word for understanding the selection, students' knowledge of and exposure to the word, the importance for future learning, students' socioeconomic status (SES), and students' English language proficiency.

Step 6   Circle the Tier 1 and Tier 3 words that are critical for comprehending the selection.

Step 7   Decide which of the circled words need only brief instruction. Enter those words in the Brief Instruction column.

Step 8   Decide which of the circled words need more elaborate instruction. Enter those words in the Elaborate Instruction column.

Step 9   If you targeted fewer than five words for brief and elaborate instruction, you will need to choose additional words from the selection. You will use Worksheet 2F: Task Analysis: Selecting Words to Teach (Teacher-Selected Words) to guide you in determining which of the additional words will require brief or elaborate instruction. The words you select will be recorded on Worksheet 2D: Selecting Words to Teach Table. Keep in mind that you should teach no more than 10 words per selection.

Step 10   Be ready to discuss the following question: How would you compare the words entered in the Brief Instruction and Elaborate Instruction columns with the words recommended by the publisher?

Discuss the Activity

Discuss the following question:

a. How would you compare the words you entered in the Brief Instruction and Elaborate Instruction columns with the words recommended by the publisher?

Plan Collaboratively

1. You will be working with another selection to determine if there is agreement with the publisher regarding which words should be taught before reading and, of those words, which will require brief instruction and which will require more elaborate instruction.

2. Make another copy of Worksheet 2D: Selecting Words to Teach Table.

3. Use the procedure from the preceding Practice the Activity section to guide you through the activity.

Assignment

There is no assignment for this session.

Selecting Words to Teach

Every day teachers make important decisions regarding what to teach and how to design effective learning experiences for their students. They know that students who have many opportunities to work with vocabulary words will have a greater chance at understanding the material they are reading. One judgment educators have to make is which words they will choose to teach before students read a selection.

Narrative and informational texts are fraught with challenging vocabulary. It would be impossible and inefficient to explicitly teach all of those words. In addition to determining the categories of natural context, there are additional factors to consider when selecting words to teach: importance, usefulness, students' prior knowledge, and the word's importance for students' future learning.

Importance

Nagy (1988) defined *Importance* as the role the word plays in the text. He identified four levels of importance: conceptually central to understanding the selection, important for understanding the gist but not central to the selection, useful but not crucial for understanding the selection, and unimportant for comprehending the critical concepts in the selection.

Conceptually central vocabulary consists of words that students will need to know in order to comprehend the key concepts in the selection. Typically, conceptually central words are taught when the meaning cannot be determined either by context (i.e., nondirective and misdirective contexts) or by analyzing its structure (i.e., affix, base word, or root word).

Usefulness

The word's usefulness or utility is another important factor to take into consideration when selecting words to teach. Beck, McKeown, and Kucan (2000) developed a system for determining the level of usefulness by classifying words into tiers. Common words that usually do not require instruction (e.g., *book, run, flower, talk*) are classified as Tier 1 words. Tier 2 words span several subject areas and are "high frequency for mature language users" (Beck et al., 2002) (e.g., *encourage, situation, enormous, volunteer*). Words that are affiliated with a specific content area are classified as Tier 3 (e.g., *carburetor, diode, binary, kurtosis*).

Student Factors

Prior Knowledge and Previous Exposure
There are two important student factors to consider when choosing words. These factors address the students' prior knowledge of or previous exposure to the word and the word's significance or importance for future learning. An effective way to determine students' knowledge of or exposure to a word is by considering the grade they are in and asking if

---

the students had previous experience with or exposure to this word. The word *amendment*, for example, appears in a chapter on the Constitution in a fifth-grade social studies text-book. The teachers know that their students have knowledge of and experience with this word from a previous unit addressing the Bill of Rights. Consequently, the definition would not have to be taught. Rather, the teachers would provide cumulative review by briefly dis-cussing the meaning during prereading activities.

Future Learning

The significance of the word for future learning is the second student factor to consider when selecting words. Blachowicz (1985) suggested that when choosing vocabulary words we should ask ourselves if the word is important for students to know 5 years from now. For example, a chapter in a fourth-grade world history textbook contains the words *environment, culture, democracy*, and *defeat*. A teacher could reason that knowing the meaning of these words would be critical for understanding concepts in future history classes. Conversely, the words *cuneiform* and *hieroglyphics* would be discussed in context as their importance for students to know in 5 years is dubious.

Summary

There are four important factors to consider when selecting words to teach before students read a selection: 1) Natural Context, 2) Importance, 3) Usefulness, and 4) Student Factors.

1. There are four categories of natural context.

    a. *Misdirective:* The context leads the reader toward the incorrect meaning of the word.

    b. *Nondirective:* The context does not assist the reader in determining the meaning of the target word.

    c. *Directive:* There is enough information to lead students to the correct meaning of the word or the word is explicitly defined/explained in the text.

    d. *General:* The context provides readers with adequate information to give them a general idea of the word's meaning.

2. Words can be categorized into four levels according to their importance in the selection.

    a. *Conceptually central*

    b. *Important*

    c. *Useful*

    d. *Unimportant*

3. Three tiers are used to describe the usefulness or utility of words:

    a. *Tier 1:* The most basic words

    b. *Tier 2:* Words found across a variety of subject areas

    c. *Tier 3:* Words specific to subject areas

4. There are two student factors to consider when selecting words to teach:

   a. Students' knowledge of or previous exposure to the word

   b. The importance of the word for current and future learning

REFERENCES

Beck, I.L., McKeown, M.G., & Kucan, L. (2002). *Bringing words to life: Robust vocabulary instruction*. New York: Guilford Press.

Blachowicz, C.L.V. (1985). Vocabulary development and reading: From research to instruction. *Reading Teacher, 38*, 876–881.

Nagy, W.E. (1988). *Vocabulary instruction and reading comprehension* (Tech. Rep. No. 431). Champaign, IL: Center for the Study of Reading, University of Illinois.

WORKSHEET 2B

Study Guide

Selecting Words to Teach

2

1. Choose a statement from Worksheet 2A: Selecting Words to Teach that you think is important and explain why.

2. Sort the following words into tiers.

justify	rain	key
solstice	intrigue	star
diode	aorta	extraordinary

Tier 1	Tier 2	Tier 3

Semantic Map

Selecting Words to Teach

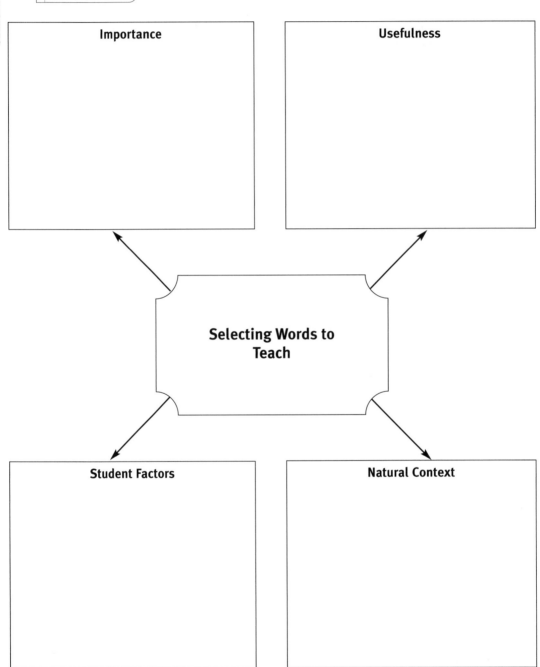

WORKSHEET 2D

Selecting Words to Teach Table

Selection: _____

Word bank		

Tier 1	Tier 2	Tier 3

Brief instruction	Elaborate instruction

Note: Remember to teach no more than 10 words per selection.

Copyright © 2009 by Paul H. Brookes Publishing Co., Inc. All rights reserved.

Cooperative Parenting

Most animals leave the frozen Antarctic ice during the winter, but the emperor penguin stays and even incubates its eggs during the coldest months. Father penguins nestle the eggs in special areas on their feet while the females hunt and feed. During the intense cold, the males remain on the ice in an *enormous* group. They trade places from the outside to the inside in order to share the warmth.

The females return after nearly two months. They listen intently to the *vociferous*, or loud and insistent, calling of the males until they hear the special sound of their own mate. When they are reunited, the male carefully moves the egg to the female's feet, and then it is his turn to hunt and eat. When the egg hatches, both parents take turns caring for the chick and spending time at sea finding food.

Task Analysis

Selecting Words to Teach (Teacher-Selected Words)

Directions: If fewer than five words were targeted for brief and elaborate instruction, choose additional words from the selection. Use the following steps for each additional word to determine if it requires brief or elaborate instruction. Teach no more than 10 words per selection.

1. Does the word belong in the misdirective or nondirective category? If so, proceed to Step 2. This word may be a candidate for the word bank. If not, proceed to the next word. Descriptions of the natural context categories are as follows:

   • Misdirective: The context leads the reader toward the incorrect meaning of the word.

   • Nondirective: The context does not assist the reader in determining the meaning of the target word.

   • Directive: There is enough information to lead the reader to the correct meaning of the word, or the word is explicitly defined or explained in the text.

   • General: The context provides the reader with adequate information to give a general idea of the word's meaning.

2. Is the word critical (i.e., conceptually central) for understanding the selection? If so, proceed to Step 3. If not, proceed to the next word.

3. Next, consider the student factors.

   a. Ask yourself if the students have had sufficient previous experience with or exposure to the word.

   b. Ask yourself if the word will be important for students to know 5 years from now.

   c. Write the word in the word bank if you decided that students have not had sufficient previous experience with or exposure to the word and it will be important for students to know 5 years from now. Repeat Steps 1–3 for the remaining words before proceeding to Step 4.

4. Determine whether each word in the word bank is a Tier 1, Tier 2, or Tier 3 word. Enter each word in the appropriate column. Descriptions of the tiers are as follows:

   - Tier 1 are the most basic words (e.g., *desk, run, house*). Students rarely need to be taught these words.

   - Tier 2 are high frequency words for mature language users and are found across a variety of subject areas (e.g., *adequate, enormous, vociferous, satisfactory*).

   - Tier 3 words are used infrequently and are often limited to a specific subject area (e.g., *chlorophyll, archipelago, diode, ventricle*).

5. Circle the Tier 2 words that are most necessary for comprehending the selection. Again, consider factors such as the importance of the word for understanding the selection, students' knowledge of and exposure to the word, the importance for future learning, socioeconomic status (SES), and English language proficiency.

6. Circle the Tier 1 and Tier 3 words that are critical for comprehending the selection.

7. Decide which of the circled words need only brief instruction. Enter those words in the Brief Instruction column.

8. Decide which of the circled words need more elaborate instruction. Enter those words in the Elaborate Instruction column.

Student Friendly Definitions

FOCUS RESEARCH CONCEPT

- Developing Student Friendly Definitions

CUMULATIVE REVIEW

- Categories of Natural Context: Misdirective, Nondirective, Directive, and General
- Selecting Words to Teach

SESSION GOALS

1. Understand the importance of providing initial word meanings through student friendly definitions.
2. Plan a lesson that includes student friendly definitions for words in the core reading program.

Overview of the Session

A key idea guiding teachers when they introduce vocabulary is to provide students with initial word meanings through student friendly definitions. In the first part of the session, you will debrief the key aspects of selecting words to teach from the previous lesson followed by a review of the focus research concept, Developing Student Friendly Definitions. Next, using Worksheet 3D: Task Analysis: Selecting Words to Teach (Words Recommended by the Publisher) and Worksheet 3E: Selecting Words to Teach Table, you will determine which of the recommended words require brief and elaborate instruction. You will review definitions for these vocabulary words and determine whether the definition provided by the publisher is student friendly. You will develop student friendly definitions for the words you selected for brief and elaborate instruction that were deemed not student friendly. Finally, if fewer than five words require brief or elaborate instruction, you will select additional words and prepare student friendly definitions for those words you selected for brief or elaborate instruction.

Debrief

During the last collaborative planning session, you were asked to choose at least one additional reading selection and determine words that require brief instruction and those that require elaborate instruction. Discuss the following questions:

- How would you compare the words you entered in the Brief Instruction and Elaborate Instruction columns with the words recommended by the publisher?

- What words did you choose that were not recommended by the publisher?

- Why did you choose those words?

- How do you think students will respond to the words you targeted for instruction?

- How did this exercise help you?

Discuss the Focus Research Concept

1. Notice the topic of this session, Student Friendly Definitions. This session will emphasize the procedures for developing student friendly definitions. Take a few minutes to read the worksheet of the focus research concept, Worksheet 3A: Student Friendly Definitions, and complete Worksheet 3B: Study Guide: Student Friendly Definitions. (See the appendix at the end of the book for the answer key to Worksheet 3B: Study Guide: Student Friendly Definitions.)

2. Discuss your answers to Study Guide Questions 1 and 2.

3. Discuss the responses you wrote in the double entry journal portion of the study guide.

4. Using Worksheet 3C: Activity: Student Friendly Definitions, evaluate the definitions to determine whether the definitions of the words for the grade level you teach are student friendly. Indicate your decision by circling Friendly or Unfriendly. Discuss how you responded.

5. Develop student friendly definitions for one or two words whose definitions were deemed unfriendly. Examples are provided in the answer key for each grade level of Worksheet 3C: Activity: Student Friendly Definitions (see the appendix at the end of the book).

Compare Research with Practice

Preview the Activity

1. The purpose of the activity in this session is to determine if the definitions for the words recommended by the publisher are student friendly. You will determine which of the recommended words will require brief instruction and which will require more elaborate instruction. Next, you will determine if each word targeted for instruction has a student friendly definition. You will use Worksheet 3D: Selecting Words to Teach (Words Recommended by the Publisher), Worksheet 3E: Selecting Words to Teach Table, Worksheet 3F: Task Analysis: Student Friendly/Not Student Friendly Definitions, and Worksheet 3G: Student Friendly/Not Student Friendly Definition Table.

2. Before you begin, consider the definition of the word *artist*. One definition of *artist* is "a person who creates art." This definition does not adequately explain the meaning of the word. Rather, it provides a general or vague description that does not give students enough information to understand the word's meaning. A student friendly definition for *artist* would be "a person who draws or paints pictures or creates sculptures as a job or hobby" (Macaulay & Seaton, 2003, p. 68). Notice that the definition focuses on specific aspects of the word's meaning and explains it in everyday language. Because the first definition of *artist* is not student friendly, it will be placed in the Not Student Friendly column on Worksheet 3G: Student Friendly/Not Student Friendly Definition Table.

Practice the Activity

1. Turn to Worksheet 3D: Task Analysis: Selecting Words to Teach (Words Recommended by the Publisher) and Worksheet 3E: Selecting Words to Teach Table. Use the task analysis to guide you through selecting words to teach.

2. Turn to Worksheet 3F: Task Analysis: Student Friendly/Not Student Friendly Definitions and Worksheet 3G: Student Friendly/Not Student Friendly Definition Table. Use the task analysis to guide you through the activity.

3. Follow the steps on the task analysis until all of the words in the Brief Instruction and Elaborate Instruction columns have been sorted into the Student Friendly or Not Student Friendly category.

Discuss the Activity

Discuss the following questions:

a. How well did the definition in the teacher's guide focus on the specific aspects of the word's meaning?

b. How well did the definition explain the meaning in everyday language?

Plan Collaboratively

1. You will now develop student friendly definitions for the words you analyzed in the Practice the Activity portion of this session.

2. Turn to Worksheet 3H: Student Friendly Definitions for Target Words.

3. Develop student friendly definitions for the words you wrote in the Not Student Friendly column (Worksheet 3G: Student Friendly/Not Student Friendly Definition Table). Write the definitions on Worksheet 3H: Student Friendly Definitions for Target Words.

4. If fewer than five words were targeted for brief and elaborate instruction, you will need to choose additional words from the selection. Use Worksheet 3I: Task Analysis: Selecting Words to Teach (Teacher-Selected Words) to guide you in determining which of the additional words will require brief or elaborate instruction. Record the words you selected on Worksheet 3E: Selecting Words to Teach Table. Teach no more than 10 words per selection.

5. Develop student friendly definitions for the words you wrote in the Brief Instruction and Elaborate Instruction columns of Worksheet 3E: Selecting Words to Teach Table. Write the definitions on Worksheet 3H: Student Friendly Definitions for Target Words.

Assignment

Teach the vocabulary using the student friendly definitions you developed.

Reference

Macaulay, A., & Seaton, M. (Eds.). (2003). *Collins cobuild advanced learner's English dictionary* (4th ed.). London: HarperCollins.

Student Friendly Definitions

One of the primary goals of vocabulary instruction is to ensure that words become part of students' listening, speaking, reading, and writing vocabularies. Toward that goal, educators should use effective vehicles that result in "deep and sustained knowledge of words" (Beck, McKeown, & Kucan Beck, 2002, p. 32). The first step in achieving this goal is developing definitions that make sense to students. Most definitions in traditional dictionaries are written in a style that does not adequately convey the meaning of the word. Consequently, using dictionary definitions sometimes gets in the way of understanding word meanings, especially to a naive learner who has little or no knowledge of the word. In fact, it has been said that dictionaries are good only if you already know the meaning of the word.

Beck and her colleagues analyzed many dictionary definitions. They identified characteristics that tend to confound rather than clarify the word's meaning. These characteristics include vague language, weak differentiation among the target word and related words, language that leads the reader to misinterpret the meaning, and definitions with multiple pieces of information that are not integrated. The *New Oxford American Dictionary* (McKean, 2005) defines *vociferous* as "vehement or clamorous." Regardless of which of Beck's characteristics this definition exemplifies, the definition does not convey specific aspects of the word's meaning in language that a person who is learning it can understand.

A student's potential for learning a word is enhanced when it is clearly defined by what is referred to as a *student friendly definition*, a term introduced into the vernacular by Beck et al. (2002). A student friendly or comprehensible definition describes a word by focusing on specific aspects of its meaning rather than providing a vague, general description. Student friendly definitions use words that are part of the students' everyday vocabulary to convey the connotation of the word. *Connotation* refers to the associations people make with a word or how it is typically used.

A student friendly definition for *vociferous* would be the following: "If you describe someone as *vociferous*, you mean that they speak with great energy and determination because they want their views to be heard" (Macaulay & Seaton, 2003, p. 1626). This definition conveys the connotation in a clear, logical fashion using words that students can understand. It does not assume that students know the meanings of difficult words such as *vehement* and *clamorous*. Rather, it distinctly conveys the word's connotation that vociferous people are *vehement* and *clamorous* because they are intent on sharing their position widely and with conviction.

Let's look at two definitions for the word *procrastinate*:

1. "To put off doing something to a future time." (*Merriam-Webster Online Dictionary*, 2009)

2. "If you procrastinate, you keep leaving things you should do until later, often because you do not want to do them" (Macaulay & Seaton, 2003, p, 1139).

For a naive learner, the connotation of *procrastinate* is more clearly conveyed in the second definition. A procrastinator puts off doing something to a future time because it is unpleasant, boring, or difficult. The first definition could lead the naive learner to think that putting off or delaying an activity for any reason is procrastinating. For example, a student might think a person is procrastinating if she puts off going to a movie she knows she would enjoy because she would rather play tennis. A student might also misconstrue the connotation of *procrastinate* in a situation where a couple delays putting an addition on to their home because they do not have the money.

Student friendly definitions should characterize the word by highlighting the specific aspects of its meaning rather than providing a general description. If a word has multiple meanings, it is not necessary to address all facets of the word during initial instruction. It is more important to concentrate on the meaning that will help students comprehend the selection at hand.

REFERENCES

Beck, I.L., McKeown, M.G., & Kucan, L. (2002). *Bringing words to life: Robust vocabulary instruction*. New York: Guilford Press.

Macaulay, A., & Seaton, M. (Eds.). (2003). *Collins cobuild advanced learner's English dictionary* (4th ed.). London: HarperCollins.

McKean, E. (Ed.). (2005). *The New Oxford American dictionary* (2nd ed.). New York: Oxford University Press.

procrastinate. (2009). In *Merriam-Webster online dictionary*. Retrieved January 20, 2009, from http://www.merriam-webster.com/dictionary/procrastinate

WORKSHEET 3B

Study Guide

Student Friendly Definitions

1. List two reasons why teachers should use student friendly definitions when teaching vocabulary.

2. What should a good dictionary definition convey?

Double Entry Journal

Directions: On the right side of the following double entry journal, write your reactions to the statements taken from Worksheet 3A: Student Friendly Definitions.

Statements	Reactions
1. Educators should use effective vehicles that result in "deep and sustained knowledge of words" (Beck, McKeown, & Kucan, 2002, p. 32).	
2. Using dictionary definitions sometimes gets in the way of understanding word meanings, especially to a naive learner who has little or no knowledge of the word.	

3

Activity

Student Friendly Definitions

First Grade

Directions: Determine whether the definitions for the following words are student friendly. Indicate your decision by circling Friendly or Unfriendly.

1. *Precious:* of great value or high price

   Friendly   Unfriendly

2. *Wonderful:* exciting

   Friendly   Unfriendly

3. *Amazing:* You say something is amazing when it is very surprising and makes you feel pleasure, approval, or wonder.

   Friendly   Unfriendly

Activity

Student Friendly Definitions

Second Grade

Directions: Determine whether the definitions for the following words are student friendly. Indicate your decision by circling Friendly or Unfriendly.

1. *Hungry:* When you are hungry you want food because you have not eaten for some time and have an uncomfortable or painful feeling in your stomach.

   Friendly   Unfriendly

2. *Protect:* to cover or shield from exposure, injury, damage, or destruction

   Friendly   Unfriendly

3. *Statue:* large sculpture modeled or carved out of a material such as stone, clay, metal, or wood

   Friendly   Unfriendly

3

Activity

Student Friendly Definitions

Third Grade

Directions: Determine whether the definitions for the following words are student friendly. Indicate your decision by circling Friendly or Unfriendly.

1. *Sensible:* of a kind to be felt or perceived: as a: perceptible to the senses or to reason or understanding

    Friendly   Unfriendly

2. *Splendid:* If you say something is splendid, you mean it is very good.

    Friendly   Unfriendly

3. *Brave:* having or showing courage

    Friendly   Unfriendly

Activity

Student Friendly Definitions

Fourth Grade

Directions: Determine whether the definitions for the following words are student friendly. Indicate your decision by circling Friendly or Unfriendly.

1. *Crime:* an act or the commission of an act that is forbidden or the omission of a duty that is commanded by a public law and that makes the offender liable to punishment by that law

   Friendly   Unfriendly

2. *Outspoken:* direct and open in speech or expression

   Friendly   Unfriendly

3. *Taunt:* what someone does if they say unkind or insulting things to you, especially about your weaknesses or failures

   Friendly   Unfriendly

Activity

Student Friendly Definitions

Fifth Grade

Directions: Determine whether the definitions for the following words are student friendly. Indicate your decision by circling Friendly or Unfriendly.

1. *Oppose:* to place over against something so as to provide resistance, counterbalance, or contrast

   Friendly   Unfriendly

2. *Disappointed:* sad because something has not happened or because something is not as good as you had hoped

   Friendly   Unfriendly

3. *Dread:* to fear greatly

   Friendly   Unfriendly

Activity

Student Friendly Definitions

Sixth Grade

Directions: Determine whether the definitions for the following words are student friendly. Indicate your decision by circling Friendly or Unfriendly.

1. *Hoax:* a trick in which someone tells people a lie (e.g., saying there is a bomb some-where when there is not, saying that a painting is genuine when it is not)

   Friendly   Unfriendly

2. *Conserve:* to keep in a safe or sound state

   Friendly   Unfriendly

3. *Amiable:* someone who is friendly and pleasant

   Friendly   Unfriendly

**WORKSHEET
3D**

Task Analysis

Selecting Words to Teach (Words Recommended by the Publisher)

Directions: Choose a selection in the core reading program. Review the words the publisher recommends teaching students before they read the selection. Read the selection. Use the following steps for each recommended word to determine if it requires brief instruction or elaborate instruction. Teach no more than 10 words per selection.

1. Does the word belong in the misdirective or nondirective category? If so, proceed to Step 2. This word may be a candidate for the word bank. If not, proceed to the next word. Descriptions of the natural context categories are as follows:

   • Misdirective: The context leads the reader toward the incorrect meaning of the word.

   • Nondirective: The context does not assist the reader in determining the meaning of the target word.

   • Directive: There is enough information to lead the reader to the correct meaning of the word, or the word is explicitly defined or explained in the text.

   • General: The context provides the reader with adequate information to give a general idea of the word's meaning.

2. Is the word critical (i.e., conceptually central) for understanding the selection? If so, proceed to Step 3. If not, proceed to the next word.

3. Next, consider the student factors.

   a. Ask yourself if the students had sufficient previous experience with or exposure to the word.

   b. Ask yourself if the word will be important for students to know 5 years from now.

   c. Write the word in the word bank if you decided that students have not had sufficient previous experience with or exposure to the word and it will be important for them to know 5 years from now. Repeat Steps 1–3 for the remaining words before proceeding to Step 4.

4. Determine whether each word in the word bank is a Tier 1, Tier 2, or Tier 3 word. Enter each word in the appropriate column. Descriptions of the tiers are as follows:

    *   Tier 1 are the most basic words (e.g., *desk, run, house*). Students rarely need to be taught these words.

    *   Tier 2 are high frequency words for mature language users and are found across a variety of subject areas (e.g., *adequate, enormous, vociferous, satisfactory*).

    *   Tier 3 words are used infrequently and are often limited to a specific subject area (e.g., *chlorophyll, archipelago, diode, ventricle*).

5. Circle the Tier 2 words that are most necessary for comprehending the selection. Again, consider such factors as the importance of the word for understanding the selection, students' knowledge of and exposure to the word, the importance for future learning, students' socioeconomic status (SES), and students' English language proficiency.

6. Circle the Tier 1 and Tier 3 words that are critical for comprehending the selection.

7. Decide which of the circled words need only brief instruction. Enter those words in the Brief Instruction column.

8. Decide which of the circled words need more elaborate instruction. Enter those words in the Elaborate Instruction column.

3

Selecting Words to Teach Table

Selection: _____

Word bank		

Tier 1	Tier 2	Tier 3

Brief instruction	Elaborate instruction

Note: Remember to teach no more than 10 words per selection.

 Learning How to Improve Vocabulary Instruction Through Teacher Study Groups by Joseph Dimino & Mary Jo Taylor
Copyright © 2009 by Paul H. Brookes Publishing Co., Inc. All rights reserved.

WORKSHEET 3F

Task Analysis

Student Friendly/Not Student Friendly Definitions

3

Directions: Use the following steps to determine whether the publisher's definitions for the words you entered in the Brief Instruction and Elaborate Instruction columns on Worksheet 3E: Selecting Words to Teach Table are student friendly.

1. Read the definition for the first word.

2. Determine whether the definition is student friendly. Indicate your decision by writing the word in either the Student Friendly or Not Student Friendly column of Worksheet 3G: Student Friendly/Not Student Friendly Definition Table.

   Student friendly definitions contain two important elements:

   • Characterize the word: Student friendly definitions describe the word by focusing on specific aspects of its meaning rather than on a general description.

   • Explain meanings in everyday language: The definition is crafted using words that are part of the student's vocabulary and convey the connotation of the word.

3. Repeat Steps 1 and 2 until all recommended words are categorized.

WORKSHEET 3G

Student Friendly/Not Student Friendly Definition Table

Selection: _____

Student friendly	Not student friendly

Learning How to Improve Vocabulary Instruction Through Teacher Study Groups by Joseph Dimino & Mary Jo Taylor
Copyright © 2009 by Paul H. Brookes Publishing Co., Inc. All rights reserved.

Student Friendly Definitions for Target Words

Target word: _____

Student friendly definition: _____

_____

_____

_____

Target word: _____

Student friendly definition: _____

_____

_____

_____

Target word: _____

Student friendly definition: _____

_____

_____

_____

Target word: _____

Student friendly definition: _____

_____

_____

_____

Target word: _____

Student friendly definition: _____

_____

_____

_____

Task Analysis

Selecting Words to Teach (Teacher-Selected Words)

Directions: If fewer than five words were targeted for brief and elaborate instruction, choose additional words from the selection. Use the following steps for each additional word to determine if it requires brief or elaborate instruction. Teach no more than 10 words per selection.

1. Does the word belong in the misdirective or nondirective category? If so, proceed to Step 2. This word may be a candidate for the word bank. If not, proceed to the next word. Descriptions of the natural context categories are as follows:

   - Misdirective: The context leads the reader toward the incorrect meaning of the word.

   - Nondirective: The context does not assist the reader in determining the meaning of the target word.

   - Directive: There is enough information to lead the reader to the correct meaning of the word, or the word is explicitly defined or explained in the text.

   - General: The context provides the reader with adequate information to give a general idea of the word's meaning.

2. Is the word critical (i.e., conceptually central) for understanding the selection? If so, proceed to Step 3. If not, proceed to the next word.

3. Next, consider the student factors.

   a. Ask yourself if the students had sufficient previous experience with or exposure to the word.

   b. Ask yourself if the word will be important for students to know 5 years from now.

   c. Write the word in the word bank if you decided that students have not had sufficient previous experience with or exposure to the word and it will be important for them to know 5 years from now. Repeat Steps 1–3 for the remaining words before proceeding to Step 4.

4. Determine whether each word in the word bank is a Tier 1, Tier 2, or Tier 3 word. Enter each word in the appropriate column. Descriptions of the tiers are as follows:

    *   Tier 1 are the most basic words (e.g., *desk, run, house*). Students rarely need to be taught these words.

    *   Tier 2 are high frequency words for mature language users and are found across a variety of subject areas (e.g., *adequate, enormous, vociferous, satisfactory*).

    *   Tier 3 words are used infrequently and are often limited to a specific subject area (e.g., *chlorophyll, archipelago, diode, ventricle*).

5. Circle the Tier 2 words that are most necessary for comprehending the selection. Again, consider such factors as the importance of the word for understanding the selection, students' knowledge of and exposure to the word, the importance for future learning, students' socioeconomic status (SES), and students' English language proficiency.

6. Circle the Tier 1 and Tier 3 words that are critical for comprehending the selection.

7. Decide which of the circled words need only brief instruction. Enter those words in the Brief Instruction column.

8. Decide which of the circled words need more elaborate instruction. Enter those words in the Elaborate Instruction column.

VOCABULARY SESSION

Examples, Nonexamples, and Concrete Representations

FOCUS RESEARCH CONCEPT

- Developing Examples, Nonexamples, and Concrete Representations

CUMULATIVE REVIEW

- Categories of Natural Context: Misdirective, Nondirective, Directive, and General
- Selecting Words to Teach
- Developing Student Friendly Definitions

SESSION GOALS

1. Learn the importance of using examples and nonexamples to pinpoint the meaning of words.
2. Develop an understanding of how concrete representations can enhance vocabulary instruction.
3. Understand the importance of using a logical instructional sequence when planning vocabulary lessons.
4. Plan vocabulary lessons that include student friendly definitions, examples, nonexamples, and concrete representations for words in the core reading program.

4

Overview of the Session

This session highlights the teacher's role in supporting students' learning by demonstrating how to develop examples and nonexamples to pinpoint the meaning of selected vocabulary words. You will learn how student friendly definitions, examples, nonexamples, and concrete representations can be embedded into a vocabulary lesson. Recall what you already know about the essential elements of good instruction: activating background knowledge, modeling/explaining, using guided practice, and using independent practice. In the first part of the session, you will debrief the vocabulary lesson you taught using the student friendly definitions you developed in the previous session. The debriefing will be followed by a review of the focus research concept, using examples, nonexamples, and concrete representations to teach words.

Next, you will determine which of the publisher's recommended words will require brief or elaborate instruction. Then you will read the definitions for these words to determine if they are student friendly and whether examples and nonexamples are included in the lesson. If they are in the lesson, you will place a checkmark in the appropriate column of Worksheet 4D: Student Friendly/Not Student Friendly, Examples, Nonexamples, Concrete Representations Table. You will look for concrete representations for the words, and indicate if they are present by placing a checkmark in the Concrete Representation column. If fewer than five words require brief or elaborate instruction you will select additional words and prepare a vocabulary lesson for these words incorporating student friendly definitions, examples, nonexamples, and concrete representations.

Debrief

During the last collaborative planning session, you developed student friendly definitions. Describe your lesson and how you thought your students responded. Provide feedback to your colleagues by responding to questions and concerns. If students' work samples were collected, examine them for strengths and weaknesses. Discuss the following questions:

- Did you find it difficult to compose student friendly definitions? Why? Why not?

- Describe the lesson you taught.

- Did you teach the lesson as planned? If not, describe any adjustments you made and why you made them.

- How did your students respond to the instruction?

- How did using student friendly definitions help students comprehend the text?

Discuss the Focus Research Concept

1. Notice the topic of this session, Examples, Nonexamples, and Concrete Representations. This session will emphasize how examples, nonexamples, and concrete representations can be used when presenting new vocabulary to

students. Take a few minutes to read the worksheet on the focus research concept, Worksheet 4A: Examples, Nonexamples, and Concrete Representations, and complete Worksheet 4B: Study Guide: Examples, Nonexamples, and Concrete Representations.

2. Discuss your answers to Questions 1 and 2 in the study guide. (See the appendix at the end of the book for the answer key to Worksheet 4B: Study Guide: Examples, Nonexamples, and Concrete Representations.)

3. Share the reactions you wrote in the Double Entry Journal portion of the study guide.

4. Effective vocabulary instruction involves using a logical sequence of steps that incorporates the following elements: activating background knowledge, modeling, explaining, and using guided and independent practice. You will complete a sorting activity to illustrate how the instructional sequence aligns with these elements. Turn to Worksheet 4C: Instructional Framework Table. This table contains three columns: Phase of Instruction, Sequence of Instruction, and Example. The information in two of the three columns, Phase of Instruction and Example, is given. Match the set of statements describing the instructional sequence with the Phase of Instruction and Example. Compare your responses with the answer key for Worksheet 4C: Instructional Framework Table (see the appendix at the end of the book).

Compare Research with Practice

Preview the Activity

1. The purpose of this activity is to determine if the definitions provided by the publisher are student friendly and if examples, nonexamples, and concrete representations are given to augment the explanation of the word. Before this analysis can begin, you will have to determine which of the publisher's recommended words will require brief or elaborate instruction.

2. After words have been selected for brief or elaborate instruction, you will determine whether the definitions of the words targeted for instruction are student friendly.

3. Before you begin, let's take a look at the publisher's definition for the word *clutching*: "When you clutch an object you hold onto it tightly because you are scared, or worried that you might lose it." This definition is student friendly because it focuses on a specific aspect of the word (holding something very tightly because you are afraid or nervous) and clearly conveys its connotation in everyday language. Because the definition is student friendly, you would write *clutching* in the Student Friendly column of Worksheet 4D: Student Friendly/Not Student Friendly, Examples, Nonexamples, Concrete Representations Table. The publisher's explanation continues: "This is a story about Russell who always loses things. In this story,

Russell runs through the airport clutching his expensive computer so he will not lose it. You may remember your mother clutching her purse as she walked through a crowd. Clutching doesn't always mean you hold onto something because you are going to lose it. A mother could clutch her child to prevent him from falling."

Because the publisher's explanation adequately supports the meaning of the word by giving examples both within and beyond the context of the story, a checkmark would be entered in the Example Within Context column. Another checkmark would be entered in the Example Beyond Context column. Note that a nonexample is not provided. A nonexample of *clutching* would be carelessly swinging an open backpack while walking through a crowded mall.

4. You will look for any concrete representations for the word. If there is evidence of concrete representations, you would place a checkmark in the Concrete Representation column.

5. There are task analyses to guide you through these activities.

Practice the Activity

1. Turn to Worksheet 4E: Task Analysis: Selecting Words to Teach (Words Recommended by the Publisher) and Worksheet 4F: Selecting Words to Teach Table. Choose a selection in the core reading program that you will be teaching before the next session. Use the task analysis to guide you through selecting words to teach.

2. Turn to Worksheet 4G: Task Analysis: Student Friendly/Not Student Friendly, Examples, Nonexamples, and Concrete Representations and Worksheet 4D: Student Friendly/Not Student Friendly, Examples, Nonexamples, Concrete Representations Table.

3. Use the task analysis to guide you through determining if the publisher's definitions were student friendly or not student friendly and to determine whether the instructional recommendations provide examples, nonexamaples, and concrete representations.

Discuss the Activity

Discuss the following questions:

a. How well did the definition in the teacher's guide focus on the specific aspects of the word's meaning?

b. How well did the definition explain the meaning in everyday language?

c. What evidence was there of examples, nonexamples, and concrete representations?

Plan Collaboratively

1. You will develop student friendly definitions, examples, nonexamples, and concrete representations for the words you entered in the Brief and Elaborate Instruction column during the Compare Research with Practice portion of the session.

2. Turn to Worksheet 4H: Vocabulary Lesson Design Framework. Follow the steps below to complete this activity. Complete one Worksheet 4H: Vocabulary Lesson Design Framework for each word in the Brief and Elaborate Instruction columns.

    Step 1   Develop student friendly definitions for the words you wrote in the Not Student Friendly column of Worksheet 4D: Student Friendly/Not Student Friendly, Examples, Nonexamples, Concrete Representations Table. Write the definitions in the Student Friendly Definition section of Worksheet 4H: Vocabulary Lesson Design Framework.

    Step 2   For some of the words in the Student Friendly and Not Student Friendly categories there was no evidence of examples and nonexamples. Develop examples and nonexamples for those words and write them in the corresponding section of Worksheet 4H: Vocabulary Lesson Design Framework.

    Step 3   For some of the defined words, there was no evidence of concrete representations. List the concrete representations you will use in the corresponding section of Worksheet 4H: Vocabulary Lesson Design Framework. Keep in mind that some words may not lend themselves to concrete representations.

    Step 4   If fewer than five words were targeted for brief and elaborate instruction, choose additional words from the selection by completing the Selecting Words to Teach activity using Worksheet 4I: Task Analysis: Selecting Words to Teach (Teacher-Selected Words). Add these words to Worksheet 4F: Selecting Words to Teach Table. Teach no more than 10 words per selection.

    Step 5   Develop student friendly definitions, examples, nonexamples, and concrete representations for the additional words you wrote in the Brief Instruction and Elaborate Instruction columns of Worksheet 4F: Selecting Words to Teach Table. Complete one Worksheet 4H: Vocabulary Lesson Design Framework for each new word. Keep in mind that some words may not lend themselves to concrete representations.

Assignment

Teach the vocabulary using the student friendly definitions, examples, nonexamples, and concrete representations you developed.

Examples, Nonexamples, and Concrete Representations

Examples

It is important to provide examples (within and beyond the context of the selection) and nonexamples for the word, after it has been explained using a student friendly definition. Incorporating student friendly definitions, examples, and nonexamples into vocabulary instruction provides a deeper understanding of words and their meanings. Examples within the context of the selection help clarify and pinpoint a word's meaning. Examples beyond the context assist students in formulating a deeper understanding of the word that is logical and unambiguous. Examples beyond the context of the selection also help students who may be inclined to limit a word's connotation to the circumstances the teacher described when introducing the word.

Before reading a selection about the Boston Tea Party, for example, students are taught the word *determined*: "If you are determined to do something, you have made a firm decision to do it and will not let anything stop you" (Macaulay & Seaton, 2003, p. 384). The teacher stresses that dumping all of that tea in the Boston Harbor was one way the colonists demonstrated how determined they were. Their intent was to show the king of England that they wanted to have a voice in the government if they were going to be expected to support it through their taxes. Although this is a good explanation, some students might limit the connotation of *determined* to mean a group attempting to pursue a goal or obtain a right from a government. In reality, a person can be determined to do anything: learn a second language, play an instrument, buy a home, stay on a diet, pursue an advanced degree, and so forth.

Incorporating Examples into Instruction

Consider a selection in which the main character, Celeste, has a problem in that she rarely completes class assignments on time. The author consistently uses the word *procrastinate* and its derivatives (e.g., *procrastinator, procrastination*) to describe Celeste's lack of planning and organization. Clearly, *procrastinate* is a word that is central to students' understanding of the story and should be taught before it is read. Effective vocabulary instruction begins with the teacher providing a student friendly definition: "If you procrastinate, you keep putting off or leaving things you should do until later, often because you do not want to do them" (Macaulay & Seaton, 2003, p. 1139). Next, the teacher gives examples for the target word.

The definition is enhanced and the connotation of *procrastinate* is clarified through the use of examples within and beyond the context of the story. In the following examples, notice how the instructional language includes the reason why these are example of the target word.

Examples within the Context of the Story

- You procrastinate when you wait until the last minute to do your homework because you probably don't like doing it. You would rather play games on Xbox, listen to your iPod, or surf the Internet.

- Some students procrastinate when it comes to completing their term papers. They begin this task the day before it is due because they find it difficult, laborious, and perhaps frustrating.

Examples Beyond the Context of the Story

- Many children do not like cleaning their bedrooms or doing other chores around the house, so they procrastinate. How many times have your parents asked if you cleaned your room yet?

- Some people procrastinate when they have to make an appointment with the dentist to get a cavity filled because they are afraid it is going to hurt. Others don't like the high pitch sound of the drill.

Nonexamples

Nonexamples are a critical feature of strong vocabulary instruction. Contrasting or nonexamples are important because they further clarify a word's meaning. These contrasting, discriminating examples help pinpoint the meaning of the word by providing instances in which the definition does not apply. Nonexamples help to solidify meanings and prevent misconceptions by explicitly telling students the attributes that are not part of the word's connotation. The following section contains nonexamples of *procrastinate*. Be sure to notice how the instructional language includes the reason why these are not examples of the target word.

Incorporating Nonexamples into Instruction

- Students usually don't procrastinate when the teacher says it is time for recess. Most students stop doing their work immediately and line up quickly and quietly when the teacher announces that it's time for recess because they like to take a break from reading, writing, and doing other classroom activities.

- Boys and girls don't procrastinate when it is time to collect their weekly allowance because they can buy things they like.

- Most adults do not procrastinate when they plan their yearly vacation. They look forward to being away from their work, so they are eager to plan a vacation where they can relax and have fun doing the things they like.

4

Concrete Representations of Words

Providing concrete representations for target words is another critical attribute of effective vocabulary instruction. Concrete representations include pictures, diagrams, gestures, facial expressions, demonstrations, objects, and so forth. When students are given a concrete representation of a word their brains are able to make a connection between language—something abstract—and something tangible. In other words, language is being translated into a real image. Teachers usually use this technique to enhance their definitions of target words. Concrete representations can also be used while providing examples and nonexamples. Review the following example and nonexample of the word *procrastinate* where concrete representations are used to augment the explanation.

Example within the Context of the Story
- You procrastinate when you wait until the last minute to do your homework because you probably don't like doing it. You would rather play games on Xbox, listen to your iPod, or surf the Internet.

Concrete Representations
- The teacher explains how procrastinating is depicted in a picture of a student who is in his bedroom surfing the Internet while piles of books and papers are on his desk.

- The teacher acts out behaviors students exhibit when they avoid completing their homework assignments (e.g., playing on the computer, talking on the phone, getting something to eat).

Nonexample
- Students usually don't procrastinate when the teacher says it is time for recess. Most students stop doing their work immediately and line up quickly and quietly when the teacher announces that it's time for recess because they like to take a break from reading, writing, and doing other classroom activities.

Concrete Representation
- The teacher demonstrates by asking the students to be the teacher and say, "Line up for recess." The teacher immediately stands up and walks to the door. After the demonstration, the teacher reviews the meaning of procrastinate and shows how her quick response to the teacher's direction is not an example of procrastinating or putting off something she does not like to do. She can explain what she likes about recess to underscore why she did not procrastinate.

- The teacher shows a picture or gives a demonstration of a student who is sitting at his desk and working diligently to illustrate a nonexample of procrastinating.

REFERENCE
Macaulay, A., & Seaton, M. (Eds.). (2003). *Collins cobuild advanced learner's English dictionary* (4th ed.). London: HarperCollins.

Study Guide

Examples, Nonexamples, and Concrete Representations

1. Why is it important to provide examples within the context of a selection?

2. Why is it important to provide examples beyond the context of the story?

   a.

   b.

3. Explain why providing contrasting examples is a critical feature of strong vocabulary instruction.

4. What is the advantage of using concrete representations of a word?

Double Entry Journal

Directions: On the right side of the following Double Entry Journal, write your reactions to the statements taken from the Worksheet 4A: Examples, Nonexamples, and Concrete Representations regarding examples and nonexamples.

Statements	Reactions
1. Examples beyond the context of the selection help students who may be inclined to limit the word's connotation to the circumstances the teacher described when introducing the word.	
2. Contrasting, discriminating examples help pinpoint the meaning of the word by providing instances in which the definition does not apply.	

Instructional Framework Table

Directions: Match the set of statements describing the instructional sequence with the phases and examples.

1. Students are given an example beyond the context of the selection with a concrete representation.

2. Students complete activities without teacher guidance.

3. Students are given an example within the context of the selection with a concrete representation.

4. The meaning of a word is explained in student friendly terms with a concrete representation.

5. The teacher leads an activity to check students' understanding of a word's meaning.

6. The teacher taps into students' prior knowledge.

7. The teacher provides a nonexample.

Instructional Framework Table

Target word: ___enormous___

Phase of instruction	Sequence of instruction	Example
Activating background		Teacher (T): Can anyone think of a time when you saw something that was really big?
Explaining/modeling		T: Something that is *enormous* is very big in size or amount. (Teacher makes a gesture with her arms.)
Explaining/modeling		T: In this story, Sydney has an exciting adventure when he takes a vacation to see the *enormous* redwood trees. He describes them as *enormous* because they are so huge. Many of them are more than 200 feet high. (Teacher shows a picture of a redwood tree.)

Phase of instruction	Sequence of instruction	Example
Explaining/modeling		T: We also use the word *enormous* when we describe a large amount of something. When we took a tour of the recycling center, we saw *enormous* amounts of old newspapers. This was an *enormous* amount because there were hundreds of stacks of newspapers. (The teacher shows a photograph she took of these stacks.)
Explaining/modeling		T: The maple trees on our school grounds are not *enormous* compared with a redwood. Mice and ants would not be described as *enormous* because they are small.
Guided practice		The teacher conducts this activity with the class: T: If any of these things I say are examples of something *enormous*, say, "*enormous*." 1. A dinosaur 2. A laptop computer 3. A mansion
Independent practice		After the lesson is taught, students are asked to complete this writing exercise as homework. Would something *enormous* fit in your pocket? Why? Why not? Would something *enormous* fit in the ocean? Why? Why not? Would something *enormous* fit in a football field? Why? Why not?

4

Student Friendly/Not Student Friendly, Examples, Nonexamples, Concrete Representations Table

Selection: _____

Student friendly	Example within context	Nonexample	Example beyond context	Concrete representation

Selection: _____

Not student friendly	Example within context	Nonexample	Example beyond context	Concrete representation

Task Analysis

Selecting Words to Teach (Words Recommended by the Publisher)

4

Directions: Choose a selection in the core reading program. Review the words the publisher recommends teaching students before they read the selection. Read the selection. Use the following steps for each recommended word to determine if it requires brief instruction or elaborate instruction. Teach no more than 10 words per selection.

1. Does the word belong in the misdirective or nondirective category? If so, proceed to Step 2. This word may be a candidate for the word bank. If not, proceed to the next word. Descriptions of the natural context categories are as follows:

    *   Misdirective: The context leads the reader toward the incorrect meaning of the word.

    *   Nondirective: The context does not assist the reader in determining the meaning of the target word.

    *   Directive: There is enough information to lead the reader to the correct meaning of the word, or the word is explicitly defined or explained in the text.

    *   General: The context provides the reader with adequate information to give a general idea of the word's meaning.

2. Is the word critical (i.e., conceptually central) for understanding the selection? If so, proceed to Step 3. If not, proceed to the next word.

3. Next, consider the student factors.

    a. Ask yourself if the students had sufficient previous experience with or exposure to the word.

    b. Ask yourself if the word will be important for students to know 5 years from now.

    c. Write the word in the word bank if you decided that students have not had sufficient previous experience with or exposure to the word and it will be important for them to know 5 years from now. Repeat Steps 1–3 for the remaining words before proceeding to Step 4.

4. Determine whether each word in the word bank is a Tier 1, Tier 2, or Tier 3 word. Enter each word in the appropriate column. Descriptions of the tiers are as follows:

    *   Tier 1 are the most basic words (e.g., *desk, run, house*). Students rarely need to be taught these words.

    *   Tier 2 are high frequency words for mature language users and are found across a variety of subject areas (e.g., *adequate, enormous, vociferous, satisfactory*).

    *   Tier 3 words are used infrequently and are often limited to a specific subject area (e.g., *chlorophyll, archipelago, diode, ventricle*).

5. Circle the Tier 2 words that are most necessary for comprehending the selection. Again, consider such factors as the importance of the word for understanding the selection, students' knowledge of and exposure to the word, the importance for future learning, students' socioeconomic status (SES), and students' English language proficiency.

6. Circle the Tier 1 and Tier 3 words that are critical for comprehending the selection.

7. Decide which of the circled words need only brief instruction. Enter those words in the Brief Instruction column.

8. Decide which of the circled words need more elaborate instruction. Enter those words in the Elaborate Instruction column.

Selecting Words to Teach Table

Selection: _____

Word bank		

Tier 1	Tier 2	Tier 3

Brief instruction	Elaborate instruction

Note: Remember to teach no more than 10 words per selection.

Copyright © 2009 by Paul H. Brookes Publishing Co., Inc. All rights reserved.

Task Analysis

Student Friendly/Not Student Friendly, Examples, Nonexamples, and Concrete Representations

Directions: Use the following steps to determine whether the publisher's definitions for the words you entered in the Brief Instruction and Elaborate Instruction columns on Worksheet 4F: Selecting Words to Teach Table are student friendly. Determine whether examples, nonexamples, and concrete representations are included.

1. Read the definition for the first recommended word.

2. Determine whether the definition is student friendly. Indicate your decision by writing the word in either the Student Friendly or Not Student Friendly column of Worksheet 4D: Student Friendly/Not Student Friendly, Examples, Nonexamples, Concrete Representations Table. Student friendly definitions contain two important elements:

   • Characterize the word: Student friendly definitions describe a word by focusing on specific aspects of its meaning rather than on a general description.

   • Explain meanings in everyday language: Definitions use words that are part of the student's vocabulary and convey the connotation of a word.

3. Now that you have decided whether the definition is student friendly, read the instructional recommendations for teaching the word. Determine whether these recommendations include examples within and beyond the context of the selection. Also, determine whether nonexamples are included. If they are present, place a checkmark in the appropriate columns using Worksheet 4D: Student Friendly/Not Student Friendly, Examples, Nonexamples, Concrete Representations Table.

4. Now that you have decided whether the definition is student friendly, and whether examples and nonexamples are present, determine if there are any concrete representations for the word. If they are present, place a checkmark in the Concrete Representation column.

5. Repeat Steps 1–4 until all recommended words have been addressed.

Vocabulary Lesson Design Framework

Target word:
Student friendly definition: Concrete representation:
Examples within context of selection: (Note: Remember to tell students why these are examples of the target word.)   Concrete representation:
Examples beyond context of selection: (Note: Remember to tell students why these are examples of the target word.)   Concrete representation:
Nonexamples: (Note: Remember to tell students why these are not examples of the target word.)   Concrete representation:

WORKSHEET 41

Task Analysis

Selecting Words to Teach (Teacher-Selected Words)

Directions: If fewer than five words were targeted for brief and elaborate instruction, choose additional words from the selection. Use the following steps for each additional word to determine if it requires brief or elaborate instruction. Teach no more than 10 words per selection.

1. Does the word belong in the misdirective or nondirective category? If so, proceed to Step 2. This word may be a candidate for the word bank. If not, proceed to the next word. Descriptions of the natural context categories are as follows:

   - Misdirective: The context leads the reader toward the incorrect meaning of the word.

   - Nondirective: The context does not assist the reader in determining the meaning of the target word.

   - Directive: There is enough information to lead the reader to the correct meaning of the word, or the word is explicitly defined or explained in the text.

   - General: The context provides the reader with adequate information to give a general idea of the word's meaning.

2. Is the word critical (i.e., conceptually central) for understanding the selection? If so, proceed to Step 3. If not, proceed to the next word.

3. Next, consider the student factors.

   a. Ask yourself if the students have had sufficient previous experience with or exposure to the word.

   b. Ask yourself if the word will be important for students to know 5 years from now.

   c. Write the word in the word bank if you decided that students have not had sufficient previous experience with or exposure to the word and it will be important for students to know 5 years from now. Repeat Steps 1–3 for the remaining words before proceeding to Step 4.

4. Determine whether each word in the word bank is a Tier 1, Tier 2, or Tier 3 word. Enter each word in the appropriate column. Descriptions of the tiers are as follows:

- Tier 1 are the most basic words (e.g., *desk, run, house*). Students rarely need to be taught these words.

- Tier 2 are high frequency words for mature language users and are found across a variety of subject areas (e.g., *adequate, enormous, vociferous, satisfactory*).

- Tier 3 words are used infrequently and are often limited to a specific subject area (e.g., *chlorophyll, archipelago, diode, ventricle*).

5. Circle the Tier 2 words that are most necessary for comprehending the selection. Again, consider factors such as the importance of the word for understanding the selection, students' knowledge of and exposure to the word, the importance for future learning, socioeconomic status (SES), and English language proficiency.

6. Circle the Tier 1 and Tier 3 words that are critical for comprehending the selection.

7. Decide which of the circled words need only brief instruction. Enter those words in the Brief Instruction column.

8. Decide which of the circled words need more elaborate instruction. Enter those words in the Elaborate Instruction column.

VOCABULARY
SESSION

Activities to Promote Word Learning

FOCUS RESEARCH CONCEPT

- Developing Activities to Promote Word Learning

CUMULATIVE REVIEW

- Categories of Natural Context: Misdirective, Nondirective, Directive, and General
- Selecting Words to Teach
- Developing Student Friendly Definitions
- Developing Examples, Nonexamples, and Concrete Representations

SESSION GOALS

1. Learn the importance of using activities to promote word learning.
2. Plan a lesson that includes student friendly definitions, examples, nonexamples, concrete representations, and activities to promote word learning.

Overview of the Session

This session focuses on ways in which teachers can develop students' knowledge and understanding of words through activities that provide multiple meaningful exposures to newly and previously learned words. In the first part of the session, you will debrief on the key aspects of developing examples, nonexamples, and concrete representations from the previous session followed by a discussion of activities to promote word learning.

You will be given additional practice in deciding if definitions are student friendly and deciding whether examples, nonexamples, and concrete representations are present by using the same procedure you learned in the previous sessions. You will 1) determine which of the words the publisher recommends teaching students before they read the selection will require brief or elaborate instruction; 2) read the definition for each of the words requiring brief or elaborate instruction to determine if they are student friendly; 3) determine whether the publisher's instructional recommendations include examples, nonexamples, and concrete representations for targeted vocabulary; and 4) determine if the publisher's instructional recommendations include activities to promote word learning. Finally, if fewer than five words that require brief or elaborate instruction were identified, you will select additional words and prepare a vocabulary lesson incorporating student friendly definitions, examples, nonexamples, concrete representations, and activities to promote word learning.

Debrief

During the last collaborative planning session, you developed student friendly definitions, examples, nonexamples, and concrete representations for words requiring brief or elaborate instruction. Describe the lesson you taught and how your students responded. Provide feedback to your colleagues by discussing questions and concerns. If work samples were collected, examine them for strengths and weaknesses. Consider the following questions to guide the discussion:

- Did you find it difficult to develop examples within and beyond the context? Why? Why Not?

- Did you find it difficult to develop nonexamples? Why? Why not?

- Describe the lesson you taught.

- Did you teach the lesson as planned? If not, describe any adjustments you made and why you made them.

- How did your students respond to the instruction?

- How did examples and nonexamples along with student friendly definitions and concrete representations help students comprehend the text?

Discuss the Focus Research Concept

1. The purpose of this session is to introduce you to a number of vocabulary activities that can be used with students.

2. Take a few minutes to read the worksheet on the focus research concept, Worksheet 5A: Activities to Promote Word Learning, and complete Worksheet 5B: Study Guide: Activities to Promote Word Learning. (See also the appendix at the end of the book for the answer key to Worksheet 5B: Study Guide: Activities to Promote Word Learning.)

3. Discuss the answers to Questions 1 and 2 in the study guide.

4. Recall that it is vital to provide frequent encounters and rich instruction that actively involve students in thinking about words. Providing activities beyond the classroom is also important to sustain word knowledge. Those ideas will be presented in Session 8.

5. Turn to Worksheet 5C: Examples of Activities to Promote Word Learning. Review the descriptions of activities. This worksheet includes descriptions of generative-type activities. They have been sorted into three categories: describing/explaining, examples/nonexamples, and relationships among words.

6. The short and dynamic activities in Worksheet 5C: Examples of Activities to Promote Word Learning are designed to engage students in processing word meanings. Select an activity. Take a few minutes to study the activity, prepare a brief explanation, and share it with the group.

Compare Research with Practice

Preview the Activity

1. The purpose of this exercise is to determine whether there are activities in the teacher's edition that allow students to interact with words. You will be choosing a selection in the core reading program that you will be teaching before the next session.

2. To begin, you will determine which of the publisher's recommended words require brief or elaborate instruction. You will use Worksheet 5E: Task Analysis: Selecting Words to Teach (Words Recommended by the Publisher) and Worksheet 5F: Selecting Words to Teach Table for this activity. After words have been selected for brief or elaborate instruction, you will determine whether the definitions of the words targeted for instruction are student friendly. You will use Worksheet 5D: Student Friendly/Not Student Friendly, Examples, Nonexamples, Concrete Representations, Activity Table to place words in either the Student Friendly or Not Student Friendly column. You will also determine whether evidence of examples, nonexamples, and concrete representations are present.

3. Finally, you will be looking for activities the publisher recommends that give students opportunities to describe and explain words, examine their relationships, and identify examples and nonexamples. These activities should be similar to those described in Worksheet 5C: Examples of Activities to Promote Word Learning.

4. There are task analyses to guide you through all of the activities.

Practice the Activity

1. Turn to Worksheet 5E: Task Analysis: Selecting Words to Teach (Words Recommended by the Publisher) and Worksheet 5F: Selecting Words to Teach Table. Use the task analysis to guide you in selecting words to teach.

2. Turn to Worksheet 5G: Task Analysis: Student Friendly/Not Student Friendly, Examples, Nonexamples, Concrete Representations, and Activities to Promote Word Learning and Worksheet 5D: Student Friendly/Not Student Friendly, Examples, Nonexamples, Concrete Representations, Activity Table.

3. Use the task analysis to sort words into the Student Friendly or Not Student Friendly categories, and then determine whether there is evidence of examples, nonexamples, and concrete representations of words. Finally, decide if there are activities that allow students to interact with these words.

Discuss the Activity

Discuss the following questions:

a. What evidence was there of student friendly definitions, examples, nonexamples, and concrete recommendations?

b. Did you find evidence of activities that allow students to interact with words? Describe them.

Plan Collaboratively

1. You will develop student friendly definitions, examples, nonexamples, and concrete representations for the words you analyzed in the Practice the Activity portion of this session. You will also develop activities that give students opportunities to interact with these words.

2. Turn to Worksheet 5H: Vocabulary Lesson Design Framework. Follow the steps below to complete this activity. Complete one Worksheet 5H: Vocabulary Lesson Design Framework for each word in the Brief and Elaborate Instruction columns.

    Step 1   Develop student friendly definitions for the words you wrote in the Not Student Friendly column of Worksheet 5D: Student Friendly/Not

Student Friendly, Examples, Nonexamples, Concrete Representations, Activity Table. Write the definitions in the Student Friendly Definition section of Worksheet 5H: Vocabulary Lesson Design Framework.

Step 2   For some of the defined words, there will be no evidence of examples, nonexamples, concrete representations, and activities that promote word learning. Develop examples, nonexamples, and concrete representations for the words you wrote in the Brief and Elaborate Instruction columns. Write this information in the corresponding sections of Worksheet 5H: Vocabulary Lesson Design Framework.

Step 3   For some of the defined words, there will be no evidence of activities that promote word learning. Develop activities for those words and write them in the corresponding sections of Worksheet 5H: Vocabulary Lesson Design Framework.

Step 4   If fewer than five words were targeted for brief and elaborate instruction, choose additional words from the selection by completing the Selecting Words to Teach activity using Worksheet 5I: Task Analysis: Selecting Words to Teach (Teacher-Selected Words). Add these words to Worksheet 5F: Selecting Words to Teach Table. Teach no more than 10 words per selection.

Step 5   Develop student friendly definitions, examples, nonexamples, and concrete representations for the additional words you wrote in the Brief and Elaborate Instruction columns of Worksheet 5F: Selecting Words to Teach Table. Write this information in the corresponding sections of Worksheet 5H: Vocabulary Lesson Design Framework. Keep in mind that some words may not lend themselves to concrete representations.

Step 6   Develop activities to promote word learning for words you wrote in the Elaborate Instruction column of Worksheet 5F: Selecting Words to Teach Table. Write this information in the appropriate sections of Worksheet 5H: Vocabulary Lesson Design Framework.

Assignment

Teach the vocabulary using student friendly definitions, examples, nonexamples, concrete representations, and the activities you developed.

5

Activities to Promote Word Learning

The research in vocabulary instruction indicates that the number of exposures to words influences students' vocabulary knowledge and text comprehension (Stahl & Fairbanks, 1986). Once students understand the connotation of a word, effective vocabulary instruction incorporates practice opportunities to help them internalize the meaning. The more practice students have to deeply process a word's meaning, the greater likelihood there is that they will remember it. Therefore, students should have multiple meaningful exposures so that words become part of their working vocabulary.

The practice opportunities that provide multiple exposures are categorized into three levels of processing: association, comprehension, and generative (Stahl, 1999). At the lowest level of difficulty are the association activities. These include memorizing definitions and activities that require students to associate a word with its meaning (e.g., matching exercises, crossword puzzles).

Comprehension processing activities involve using the definitional information to classify words into categories or to complete graphic organizers such as semantic feature analysis grids (Anders & Bos, 1986; Bos & Anders, 1990), word maps, concept maps, and so forth.

Activities at the highest level of difficulty, generative processing, require students to use information to develop a new product or construct a unique, inventive response. Beck, Perfetti, and McKeown (1982) and Beck, McKeown, and Kucan (2002) developed a variety of these innovative, generative activities. The purpose was to increase vocabulary knowledge, pique students' interest, and review and reinforce previously learned words. Examples include comparing semantically related words (e.g., Would you *dread* something *appetizing*? Why? Why not?), completing sentences to demonstrate understanding of the meaning of words (e.g., The child was *forbidden* to play with the matches because . . .), or making associations among words from the text (e.g., If a child refuses to put away his toys every time his mother asks him, is he *persistent* or *compliant*? Why?).

A critical component in many of these generative activities is that students will need to justify their responses. In the activity highlighting the target words, *dread* and *appetizing*, students demonstrate understanding of the target words by defending their responses to the question, "Would you *dread* something *appetizing*?" If a justification makes sense, a variety of answers are acceptable. A common, appropriate justification would be, "No, because I wouldn't be reluctant or frightened to eat something that looks good, smells good, and probably tastes good." Conversely, an appropriate, yet dichotomous, response would be, "Yes, I would be reluctant to eat something that smells good if I am on a diet because I would be afraid that I couldn't eat just one, and I would gain weight."

Clearly, these activities require students to demonstrate their understanding of the word rather than parroting definitions, using words in sentences that may not convey an understanding of the concept, or memorizing definitions so they can complete a matching activity or a crossword puzzle.

REFERENCES

Anders, P., & Bos, C. (1986). Semantic feature analysis: An interactive strategy for vocabulary development and text comprehension. *Journal of Reading, 39*, 610–616.

Bos, C.S., & Anders, P.L. (1990). Effects of interactive vocabulary instruction on the vocabulary learning and reading comprehension of junior-high learning disabled students. *Learning Disability Quarterly, 13*, 31–42.

Beck, I.L., McKeown, M.G., & Kucan, L. (2002). *Bringing words to life: Robust vocabulary instruction*. New York: Guilford Press.

Beck, I.L., Perfetti, C.A., & McKeown, M.G. (1982). Effects of long-term vocabulary instruction on lexical access and reading comprehension. *Journal of Educational Psychology, 74*, 506–521.

Stahl, S.A. (1999). *Vocabulary development*. Newton Upper Falls, MA: Brookline.

Stahl, S.A., & Fairbanks, M.M. (1986). The effects of vocabulary instruction: A model-based meta-analysis. *Review of Educational Research, 56*, 72–110.

5

**WORKSHEET
5B**

Study Guide

Activities to Promote Word Learning

1. Describe the three levels of processing categorized by Stahl (1999).

2. What is the advantage of using activities that require students to use generative processing over those that only require processing at the association or comprehension levels?

Examples of Activities to Promote Word Learning

(Source: Beck, McKeown, & Kucan, 2002)

Describing/Explaining

1. **Word Associations** requires students to associate a known word with a newly learned word to reinforce the meaning of the new word and to promote cumulative review. This helps students embed the newly learned words into their vocabulary. Examples of word associations include the following for the words *murmur, benevolent, fragrant*, and *vociferous*:

    a.   Which word goes with *flowers*? Why?

    b.   Which word goes with *whisper*? Why?

    c.   Which word goes with *helping*? Why?

    d.   Which word goes with *loud*? Why?

2. **"Have You Ever...?"** helps students associate newly learned words based on their background knowledge and experiences. Examples of this include the following:

    a.   When might you *contradict* someone?

    b.   When might you *waver* in your decision?

    c.   When might you *criticize* something?

3. **Applause** directs students to indicate, by the volume of their clapping, how much they would like to be described by the words presented (i.e., not very much, a little, very much). Students are asked to explain why they would feel that way. Examples include the following:

    a.   Alert

    b.   Impudent

    c.   Visible

    d.   Headstrong

4. **Idea Completion** expects students to incorporate a word's meaning into a context to explain a situation. Examples of idea completion include the following:

   a. The small child was *forbidden* to play with the matches because...

   b. Right before Sarah made her debut in the dance recital, she *scanned* the audience to...

   Variations of Idea Completion examples include the following:

   a. Would you want a *frail* person on your football team? Why? Why not?

   b. What might cause an entire classroom of math students to be *baffled*?

   c. When might you need a *navigator*?

   d. When might you *cease* your activity?

   e. Why might you *wince*?

   f. What would make you feel *timid*? Why?

   g. Do you ever feel *alert*? When? Why?

   h. Have you ever been *persistent*? What happened?

5. **Questions, Reasons, and Examples** provides opportunities for students to interact with target words by responding to questions and giving examples. Examples include the following:

   a. Why is it good to *contemplate* the possible consequences of your behavior?

   b. What could you say to *convince* your parents to let you have a dog?

   c. What is something you would *boycott* in protest of low wages for farm workers?

   d. Which of the following might be *appetizing*? Why?

   The scent of flowers or the smell of chocolate?

   The smell of freshly baked cookies or grass that has just been cut?

   The smell of pizza or burning wood?

6. **Multiple Meanings** gives students practice in applying various meanings to the same word. Examples include the following:

   a. Word: *litter*

   What does the word *litter* mean to a veterinarian, a custodian, and a medic?

   b. Word: *scent*

   What does the word *scent* mean to a chef and a bloodhound?

   c. Word: *crescent*

   What does the word *crescent* mean to a baker, an astronomer, and a mapmaker?

Examples/Nonexamples

1. **Making Choices** encourages students to make choices and justify responses about a word's meaning. Examples include the following:

   a. If any of the following might make someone experience *dread*, say, "dread." Be ready to explain your answer.

   Getting a new puppy

   Hearing a strange noise

   Taking a big test

   Writing a thank you note

   Looking over the edge of a canyon

   b. I'll say some things. If they sound *impudent*, say, "impudent." If they sound *courteous*, say "courteous." Be ready to explain your answer.

   No, thank you.

   That's not the way you pronounce it!

   My mom can cook better than you can.

   May I have some more?

   You didn't give me as much as you gave her!

   c. If any of the things I say might be examples of *philanthropy* say, "philanthropy." If not, don't say anything. Be ready to explain your answer.

   Helping to feed the children of Somalia

   Giving money to your children to help them buy a house

   Helping with a fundraiser to fight breast cancer

   Donating money to a school club in exchange for advertising your company's business

   Donating money to help eradicate malaria and river blindness

   d. If a dog is *timid*, would you pet it or leave it alone? Why?

   e. Is *forage* something your brother would do or something your rabbit would do? Why?

   f. If you had a *sufficient* number of cards, would your deck be complete? Why? Why not?

   g. What would make you feel *indignant*, being chosen for the neighborhood baseball team or being left off of the invitation list for a birthday party? Why?

2. **Child-Created Examples** requires students to create examples that demonstrate their thinking about how the word relates to their background knowledge and life experiences. Examples include the following:

   a.   If your parents set up *consequences* for your poor behavior, what might they be?

   b.   If your sister persisted in *embarrassing* you in front of your friends, how would you respond?

3. **Facets of Word Meaning** stimulates a discussion among students about the critical features of a word's meaning. In this activity, students choose and justify the example that illustrates a word's connotation. Examples include the following:

   a.   Word: *persist*

   During a car trip, a child asks every mile, "Are we there yet?"

   At a rest stop, a child asks for a soda.

   b.   Word: *verify*

   You need to complete any assignments missed during absences.

   You need to bring a note from your parents when you are absent.

   c.   Word: *commitment*

   The skater continued with her lessons, practicing five days a week for several hours each day, until the time of the competition.

   Sam practices his trumpet every chance he gets, but his schedule is quite hectic so he rarely gets to it every day.

   d.   Word: *vicariously*

   The mother felt as if she, rather than her daughter, was having an operation to repair her broken arm.

   The mother sat in the operating room worried as she awaited the results of her daughter's surgery.

Relationships Among Words

Using All of the Words

It is important to develop practice items that include all target words from the selection being read. In the following activity under the subtopic Sentences, all of the words can be incorporated into one practice item or sentence; however, often it is difficult to find a relationship among all of the target words that can fit easily into one thought or idea. The activities titled Choices and One Context for All of the Words illustrate how to develop practice items in cases where all of the target words cannot easily be incorporated into one sentence.

1. **Relating Words** encourages students to explain and justify their responses to questions and choose words that fit the descriptions given in the sentence. Examples include the following:

   a. Using two words

      Would you *dread* something *appetizing*? Why? Why not?

      When does the moon *cease* being *visible*?

      When might you *verify* a *presumption*?

      If you were in *excruciating* pain, would you *wince*? Why? Why not?

   b. Sentences

      Target words from the selection: *waver, contemplating, sufficient, sacrifice, cease*

      Would you *waver* while *contemplating* sharing cookies with your brother if you thought there was not a *sufficient* number, or would you *sacrifice* some cookies to *cease* arguing? Why?

   c. Choices

      Target words from the selection: *timid, compliant, persistent, frail*

      If you do not want to go to a beach party because there are too many new people to meet, are you *frail* or *timid*? Why?

      If a child refuses to put away his things every time his mother asks him, is he *persistent* or *compliant*? Why?

2. **One Context for All of the Words** promotes students' thinking about the relationship among target words in a selection by asking questions that require knowledge of the words. In the following examples, the words *procrastinate, ramifications*, and *justify* are used in the context of situations involving homework.

   a. Why would you *procrastinate* doing your homework?

   b. What would be the *ramifications* of not doing your homework?

   c. How would you *justify* not completing your homework?

Assessment

Assessments are used to measure students' knowledge of words. The most common format is multiple choice. The previously described activities that promote multiple meaningful exposures can also be used as a valid way to assess a student's acquisition of vocabulary. Following are a few more examples:

ACTIVITIES TO PROMOTE WORD LEARNING

1. **Describing/Explaining**

   a.   Describe how someone behaves that shows he or she is *indignant*.

   b.   Tell about a time you were *baffled*.

   c.   Explain a situation that might make someone *wince*.

   d.   Mom was excited when she realized that not only was her son accepted by one of the most *prestigious* universities in the country, but he had also been given a full scholarship for the entire time he will be attending. Explain why Mom was so elated.

   e.   Place the following phrases on the word line from Little Endurance to Great Deal of Endurance and explain your placement. How much endurance does it take to . . .

   be a spectator at a *decathlon*?

   undergo an *appendectomy*?

   tolerate a child who is having a *tantrum*?

   listen to a *tedious* speaker for over an hour?

   Little Endurance .... Great Deal of Endurance

   f.   Place the following phrases on the word line from A Little Anxious to Very Anxious and explain your placement. How anxious would you be if . . .

   you were waiting to see if you received the *position* you wanted?

   airport officials just announced that the mechanical *malfunction* was repaired and the flight would be leaving as scheduled?

   the results of the contest were just about to be *conveyed* to the participants?

   your passport was *invalid*?

   A Little Anxious .... Very Anxious

2. **Relationships Among Words**

   What is alike and/or different between these pairs of words? Explain.

   headstrong/persistent

   timid/frail

   dread/dismay

   waver/baffled

3. **Examples/Nonexamples**

Beat the Clock: Give students 90 seconds to complete 14 items. This activity assesses the students' ability to quickly access words' meanings.

a.	*Timid* mice stay out of sight.	True	False
b.	*Impudent* children are welcome everywhere.	True	False
c.	*Persistent* people give up easily.	True	False
d.	Success is a *consequence* of hard work.	True	False
e.	It is impolite to *stare* at people.	True	False
f.	A restaurant has *sufficient* food.	True	False
g.	The moon is never shaped like a *crescent*.	True	False
h.	The black piano keys were *ebony*.	True	False
i.	The garden is *fragrant* in winter.	True	False
j.	The teacher was *indignant* at my *impudence*.	True	False
k.	Edison *persisted* until he created a light bulb.	True	False
l.	The players *disperse* during Hide and Seek.	True	False
m.	The teacher *presumes* we will fail our test.	True	False
n.	Grandpa was *frail* while recovering from surgery.	True	False

REFERENCE

Beck, I.L., McKeown, M.G., & Kucan, L. (2002). *Bringing words to life: Robust vocabulary instruction*. New York: Guilford Press.

5

Student Friendly/Not Student Friendly, Examples, Nonexamples, Concrete Representations, Activity Table

Selection: _____

Student friendly	Example within context	Nonexample	Example beyond context	Concrete representation	Activity

Selection: _____

Not Student friendly	Example within context	Nonexample	Example beyond context	Concrete representation	Activity

Task Analysis

Selecting Words to Teach (Words Recommended by the Publisher)

Directions: Choose a selection in the core reading program. Review the words the publisher recommends teaching students before they read the selection. Read the selection. Use the following steps for each recommended word to determine if it requires brief instruction or elaborate instruction. Teach no more than 10 words per selection.

1. Does the word belong in the misdirective or nondirective category? If so, proceed to Step 2. This word may be a candidate for the word bank. If not, proceed to the next word. Descriptions of the natural context categories are as follows:

    • Misdirective: The context leads the reader toward the incorrect meaning of the word.

    • Nondirective: The context does not assist the reader in determining the meaning of the target word.

    • Directive: There is enough information to lead the reader to the correct meaning of the word, or the word is explicitly defined or explained in the text.

    • General: The context provides the reader with adequate information to give a general idea of the word's meaning.

2. Is the word critical (i.e., conceptually central) for understanding the selection? If so, proceed to Step 3. If not, proceed to the next word.

3. Next, consider the student factors.

    a. Ask yourself if the students had sufficient previous experience with or exposure to the word.

    b. Ask yourself if the word will be important for students to know 5 years from now.

    c. Write the word in the word bank if you decided that students have not had sufficient previous experience with or exposure to the word and it will be important for them to know 5 years from now. Repeat Steps 1–3 for the remaining words before proceeding to Step 4.

4. Determine whether each word in the word bank is a Tier 1, Tier 2, or Tier 3 word. Enter each word in the appropriate column. Descriptions of the tiers are as follows:

- Tier 1 are the most basic words (e.g., *desk, run, house*). Students rarely need to be taught these words.

- Tier 2 are high frequency words for mature language users and are found across a variety of subject areas (e.g., *adequate, enormous, vociferous, satisfactory*).

- Tier 3 words are used infrequently and are often limited to a specific subject area (e.g., *chlorophyll, archipelago, diode, ventricle*).

5. Circle the Tier 2 words that are most necessary for comprehending the selection. Again, consider such factors as the importance of the word for understanding the selection, students' knowledge of and exposure to the word, the importance for future learning, students' socioeconomic status (SES), and students' English language proficiency.

6. Circle the Tier 1 and Tier 3 words that are critical for comprehending the selection.

7. Decide which of the circled words need only brief instruction. Enter those words in the Brief Instruction column.

8. Decide which of the circled words need more elaborate instruction. Enter those words in the Elaborate Instruction column.

WORKSHEET 5F

Selecting Words to Teach Table

Selection: _____

Word bank		

Tier 1	Tier 2	Tier 3

Brief instruction	Elaborate instruction

Note: Remember to teach no more than 10 words per selection.

Learning How to Improve Vocabulary Instruction Through Teacher Study Groups by Joseph Dimino & Mary Jo Taylor   103
Copyright © 2009 by Paul H. Brookes Publishing Co., Inc. All rights reserved.

5

Task Analysis

*Student Friendly/Not Student
Friendly, Examples,
Nonexamples, Concrete
Representations, and Activities
to Promote Word Learning*

Directions: Use the following steps to determine whether the publisher's definitions for the words you entered in the Brief and Elaborate Instruction columns are student friendly or not student friendly and whether the instructional recommendations include examples, nonexamples, concrete representations, and activities to promote word learning.

1. Read the definition for the first recommended word.

2. Determine whether the definition is student friendly. Indicate your decision by writing the word in either the Student Friendly or Not Student Friendly column of Worksheet 5D: Student Friendly/Not Student Friendly, Examples, Nonexamples, Concrete Representations, Activity Table. Student friendly definitions contain two important elements:

    *   Characterize the word: Student friendly definitions describe a word by focusing on specific aspects of its meaning rather than on a general description.

    *   Explain meanings in everyday language: Definitions use words that are part of the student's vocabulary and convey the connotation of a word.

3. Now that you have decided whether the definition is student friendly, read the instructional recommendations for teaching the word. Determine whether these recommendations include examples within and beyond the context of the selection. Also, determine whether nonexamples, concrete representations, and activities that give students the opportunity to interact with words are included. If they are present, place a checkmark in the appropriate columns using Worksheet 5D: Student Friendly/Not Student Friendly, Examples, Nonexamples, Concrete Representations, Activity Table.

4. Repeat Steps 1–3 until you address all recommended words.

Target word:

Student friendly definition: Concrete representation:

Examples within context of selection: (Note: Remember to tell students why these are examples of the target word.) Concrete representation:

Examples beyond context of selection: (Note: Remember to tell students why these are examples of the target word.) Concrete representation:

Nonexamples: (Note: Remember to tell students why these are not examples of the target word.) Concrete representation:

Learning How to Improve Vocabulary Instruction Through Teacher Study Groups by Joseph Dimino & Mary Jo Taylor   105
Copyright © 2009 by Paul H. Brookes Publishing Co., Inc. All rights reserved.

ACTIVITIES TO PROMOTE WORD LEARNING

Activity 1 to promote word learning

Activity 2 to promote word learning

Learning How to Improve Vocabulary Instruction Through Teacher Study Groups by Joseph Dimino & Mary Jo Taylor
Copyright © 2009 by Paul H. Brookes Publishing Co., Inc. All rights reserved.

Task Analysis

Selecting Words to Teach (Teacher-Selected Words)

Directions: If fewer than five words were targeted for brief and elaborate instruction, choose additional words from the selection. Use the following steps for each additional word to determine if it requires brief or elaborate instruction. Teach no more than 10 words per selection.

1. Does the word belong in the misdirective or nondirective category? If so, proceed to Step 2. This word may be a candidate for the word bank. If not, proceed to the next word. Descriptions of the natural context categories are as follows:

    - Misdirective: The context leads the reader toward the incorrect meaning of the word.

    - Nondirective: The context does not assist the reader in determining the meaning of the target word.

    - Directive: There is enough information to lead the reader to the correct meaning of the word, or the word is explicitly defined or explained in the text.

    - General: The context provides the reader with adequate information to give a general idea of the word's meaning.

2. Is the word critical (i.e., conceptually central) for understanding the selection? If so, proceed to Step 3. If not, proceed to the next word.

3. Next, consider the student factors.

    a. Ask yourself if the students have had sufficient previous experience with or exposure to the word.

    b. Ask yourself if the word will be important for students to know 5 years from now.

    c. Write the word in the word bank if you decided that students have not had sufficient previous experience with or exposure to the word and it will be important for students to know 5 years from now. Repeat Steps 1–3 for the remaining words before proceeding to Step 4.

4. Determine whether each word in the word bank is a Tier 1, Tier 2, or Tier 3 word. Enter each word in the appropriate column. Descriptions of the tiers are as follows:

    -   Tier 1 are the most basic words (e.g., *desk, run, house*). Students rarely need to be taught these words.

    -   Tier 2 are high frequency words for mature language users and are found across a variety of subject areas (e.g., *adequate, enormous, vociferous, satisfactory*).

    -   Tier 3 words are used infrequently and are often limited to a specific subject area (e.g., *chlorophyll, archipelago, diode, ventricle*).

5. Circle the Tier 2 words that are most necessary for comprehending the selection. Again, consider factors such as the importance of the word for understanding the selection, students' knowledge of and exposure to the word, the importance for future learning, socioeconomic status (SES), and English language proficiency.

6. Circle the Tier 1 and Tier 3 words that are critical for comprehending the selection.

7. Decide which of the circled words need only brief instruction. Enter those words in the Brief Instruction column.

8. Decide which of the circled words need more elaborate instruction. Enter those words in the Elaborate Instruction column.

Cumulative Review I

CUMULATIVE REVIEW

- Categories of Natural Context: Misdirective, Nondirective, Directive, and General
- Selecting Words to Teach
- Developing Student Friendly Definitions
- Developing Examples, Nonexamples, and Concrete Representations
- Developing Activities to Promote Word Learning

SESSION GOALS

1. Plan a lesson that includes student friendly definitions, examples, nonexamples, concrete representations, and activities that promote word learning.

Overview of the Session

This session is a cumulative review of the major research concepts addressed in the five previous sessions. Participants will put it all together by completing activities similar to those in Sessions 2–5. The activities will include practice in determining which of the publisher's recommended words will require brief or elaborate instruction followed by an activity to determine whether the instructional recommendations for those words include student friendly definitions, examples, nonexamples, concrete representations, and activities that promote word learning. You will also develop a vocabulary lesson that incorporates these components.

Debrief

During the last collaborative planning session, you were asked to develop student friendly definitions, examples, nonexamples, concrete representations, and activities that promote word learning.

Describe the lesson you taught and how you thought your students responded. Consider the following questions to guide the discussion:

- Did you find it difficult to develop activities that gave students opportunities to interact with words? Why? Why not?

- Describe one activity you taught.

- Did you teach the lesson as planned? If not, describe any adjustments you made and why you made them.

- How did your students respond to the activities you used in this lesson?

Review the Focus Research Concept

The purpose of this session is to review and practice applying the research concepts presented in the previous sessions; therefore, no new research will be discussed.

Compare Research with Practice

Preview the Activity

1. The purpose of this activity is to review and practice applying the research concepts presented in the previous sessions. You will put it all together by determining which of the publisher's recommended words will require brief or elaborate instruction followed by activities to determine which of these words include student friendly definitions, examples, nonexamples, concrete representations, and activities that promote word learning.

2. You will need the following worksheets for these activities:

    - Worksheet 6A: Task Analysis: Selecting Words to Teach (Words Recommended by the Publisher)

- Worksheet 6B: Selecting Words to Teach Table

- Worksheet 6C: Task Analysis: Student Friendly/Not Student Friendly, Examples, Nonexamples, Concrete Representations, and Activities to Promote Word Learning

- Worksheet 6D: Student Friendly/Not Student Friendly, Examples, Nonexamples, Concrete Representations, Activity Table

Practice the Activity

1. Turn to Worksheet 6A: Task Analysis: Selecting Words to Teach (Words Recommended by the Publisher) and Worksheet 6B: Selecting Words to Teach Table. Use the task analysis to guide you in selecting words to teach.

2. Turn to Worksheet 6C: Task Analysis: Student Friendly/Not Student Friendly, Examples, Nonexamples, Concrete Representations, and Activities to Promote Word Learning and Worksheet 6D: Student Friendly/Not Student Friendly, Examples, Nonexamples, Concrete Representations, Activity Table. Use the task analysis to sort words you selected for brief or elaborate instruction into the Student Friendly/Not Friendly categories, and determine whether the publisher's instructional recommendations include examples, nonexamples, concrete representation, and activities that promote word learning.

Discuss the Activity

Discuss the following questions:

a. What evidence was there of student friendly definitions, examples, nonexamples, and concrete recommendations?

b. Did you find evidence of activities that allow students to interact with words? Describe them.

Plan Collaboratively

1. You will develop student friendly definitions, examples, nonexamples, and concrete representations for the words you analyzed in the Practice the Activity portion of this lesson. You will also develop activities that give students opportunities to interact with those words (see Worksheet 6E: Examples of Activities to Promote Word Learning).

2. Turn to Worksheet 6F: Vocabulary Lesson Design Framework. Complete one Worksheet 6F: Vocabulary Lesson Design Framework for each word in the Brief and Elaborate Instruction columns.

3. Develop student friendly definitions for the words you wrote in the Not Student Friendly column of Worksheet 6D: Student Friendly/Not Student Friendly, Examples, Nonexamples, Concrete Representations, Activity Table. Write the definitions in the Student Friendly Definition section of Worksheet 6F: Vocabulary Lesson Design Framework.

4. For some of the defined words, there will be no evidence of examples, nonexamples, concrete representations, and activities that promote word learning. Develop student friendly definitions, examples, nonexamples, and concrete representation for the words you wrote in the Brief and Elaborate Instruction columns. Develop activities for the words you wrote in the Elaborate Instruction column. Write this information in the corresponding sections of Worksheet 6F: Vocabulary Lesson Design Framework.

5. If fewer than five words were targeted for brief and elaborate instruction, choose additional words from the selection by completing the Selecting Words to Teach activity using Worksheet 6G: Task Analysis: Selecting Words to Teach (Teacher-Selected Words). Add these words to Worksheet 6B: Selecting Words to Teach Table. Teach no more than 10 words per selection.

6. Develop student friendly definitions, examples, nonexamples, and concrete representations for the additional words you wrote in the Brief and Elaborate Instruction columns of Worksheet 6B: Selecting Words to Teach Table. Write this information in the corresponding sections of Worksheet 6F: Vocabulary Lesson Design Framework. Keep in mind that some words may not lend themselves to concrete representations.

7. Develop activities for the words you wrote in the Elaborate Instruction column of Worksheet 6B: Selecting Words to Teach Table. Write this information in the appropriate sections of Worksheet 6F: Vocabulary Lesson Design Framework.

Assignment

Teach the vocabulary using student friendly definitions, examples, nonexamples, concrete representations, and the activities you developed.

Task Analysis

Selecting Words to Teach (Words Recommended by the Publisher)

Directions: Choose a selection in the core reading program. Review the words the publisher recommends teaching students before they read the selection. Read the selection. Use the following steps for each recommended word to determine if it requires brief instruction or elaborate instruction. Teach no more than 10 words per selection.

1. Does the word belong in the misdirective or nondirective category? If so, proceed to Step 2. This word may be a candidate for the word bank. If not, proceed to the next word. Descriptions of the natural context categories are as follows:

    *   Misdirective: The context leads the reader toward the incorrect meaning of the word.

    *   Nondirective: The context does not assist the reader in determining the meaning of the target word.

    *   Directive: There is enough information to lead the reader to the correct meaning of the word, or the word is explicitly defined or explained in the text.

    *   General: The context provides the reader with adequate information to give a general idea of the word's meaning.

2. Is the word critical (i.e., conceptually central) for understanding the selection? If so, proceed to Step 3. If not, proceed to the next word.

3. Next, consider the student factors.

    a. Ask yourself if the students had sufficient previous experience with or exposure to the word.

    b. Ask yourself if the word will be important for students to know 5 years from now.

    c. Write the word in the word bank if you decided that students have not had sufficient previous experience with or exposure to the word and it will be important for them to know 5 years from now. Repeat Steps 1–3 for the remaining words before proceeding to Step 4.

4. Determine whether each word in the word bank is a Tier 1, Tier 2, or Tier 3 word. Enter each word in the appropriate column. Descriptions of the tiers are as follows:

- Tier 1 are the most basic words (e.g., *desk, run, house*). Students rarely need to be taught these words.

- Tier 2 are high frequency words for mature language users and are found across a variety of subject areas (e.g., *adequate, enormous, vociferous, satisfactory*).

- Tier 3 words are used infrequently and are often limited to a specific subject area (e.g., *chlorophyll, archipelago, diode, ventricle*).

5. Circle the Tier 2 words that are most necessary for comprehending the selection. Again, consider such factors as the importance of the word for understanding the selection, students' knowledge of and exposure to the word, the importance for future learning, students' socioeconomic status (SES), and students' English language proficiency.

6. Circle the Tier 1 and Tier 3 words that are critical for comprehending the selection.

7. Decide which of the circled words need only brief instruction. Enter those words in the Brief Instruction column.

8. Decide which of the circled words need more elaborate instruction. Enter those words in the Elaborate Instruction column.

Selecting Words to Teach Table

Selection: _____

Word bank		

Tier 1	Tier 2	Tier 3

Brief instruction	Elaborate instruction

Note: Remember to teach no more than 10 words per selection.

Copyright © 2009 by Paul H. Brookes Publishing Co., Inc. All rights reserved.

Task Analysis

Student Friendly/Not Student Friendly, Examples, Nonexamples, Concrete Representations, and Activities to Promote Word Learning

Directions: Use the following steps to determine whether the publisher's definitions for the words you entered in the Brief and Elaborate Instruction columns are student friendly or not student friendly and whether the instructional recommendations include examples, nonexamples, concrete representations, and activities to promote word learning.

1. Read the definition for the first recommended word.

2. Determine whether the definition is student friendly. Indicate your decision by writing the word in either the Student Friendly or Not Student Friendly column of Worksheet 5D: Student Friendly/Not Student Friendly, Examples, Nonexamples, Concrete Representations, Activity Table. Student friendly definitions contain two important elements:

   • Characterize the word: Student friendly definitions describe a word by focusing on specific aspects of its meaning rather than on a general description.

   • Explain meanings in everyday language: Definitions use words that are part of the student's vocabulary and convey the connotation of a word.

3. Now that you have decided whether the definition is student friendly, read the instructional recommendations for teaching the word. Determine whether these recommendations include examples within and beyond the context of the selection. Also, determine whether nonexamples, concrete representations, and activities that give students the opportunity to interact with words are included. If they are present, place a checkmark in the appropriate columns using Worksheet 5D: Student Friendly/Not Student Friendly, Examples, Nonexamples, Concrete Representations, Activity Table.

4. Repeat Steps 1–3 until you address all recommended words.

WORKSHEET 6D

Student Friendly/Not Student Friendly, Examples, Nonexamples, Concrete Representations, Activity Table

6

Selection: _____

Student friendly	Example within context	Nonexample	Example beyond context	Concrete representation	Activity

Selection: _____

Not Student friendly	Example within context	Nonexample	Example beyond context	Concrete representation	Activity

6

Examples of Activities to Promote Word Learning

(Source: Beck, McKeown, & Kucan, 2002)

Describing/Explaining

1. **Word Associations** requires students to associate a known word with a newly learned word to reinforce the meaning of the new word and to promote cumulative review. This helps students embed the newly learned words into their vocabulary. Examples of word associations include the following for the words *murmur, benevolent, fragrant*, and *vociferous*:

    a.   Which word goes with *flowers*? Why?

    b.   Which word goes with *whisper*? Why?

    c.   Which word goes with *helping*? Why?

    d.   Which word goes with *loud*? Why?

2. **"Have You Ever...?"** helps students associate newly learned words based on their background knowledge and experiences. Examples of this include the following:

    a.   When might you *contradict* someone?

    b.   When might you *waver* in your decision?

    c.   When might you *criticize* something?

3. **Applause** directs students to indicate, by the volume of their clapping, how much they would like to be described by the words presented (i.e., not very much, a little, very much). Students are asked to explain why they would feel that way. Examples include the following:

    a.   Alert

    b.   Impudent

    c.   Visible

    d.   Headstrong

4. **Idea Completion** expects students to incorporate a word's meaning into a context to explain a situation. Examples of idea completion include the following:

   a. The small child was *forbidden* to play with the matches because...

   b. Right before Sarah made her debut in the dance recital, she *scanned* the audience to...

   Variations of Idea Completion examples include the following:

   a. Would you want a *frail* person on your football team? Why? Why not?

   b. What might cause an entire classroom of math students to be *baffled*?

   c. When might you need a *navigator*?

   d. When might you *cease* your activity?

   e. Why might you *wince*?

   f. What would make you feel *timid*? Why?

   g. Do you ever feel *alert*? When? Why?

   h. Have you ever been *persistent*? What happened?

5. **Questions, Reasons, and Examples** provides opportunities for students to interact with target words by responding to questions and giving examples. Examples include the following:

   a. Why is it good to *contemplate* the possible consequences of your behavior?

   b. What could you say to *convince* your parents to let you have a dog?

   c. What is something you would *boycott* in protest of low wages for farm workers?

   d. Which of the following might be *appetizing*? Why?

   The scent of flowers or the smell of chocolate?

   The smell of freshly baked cookies or grass that has just been cut?

   The smell of pizza or burning wood?

6. **Multiple Meanings** gives students practice in applying various meanings to the same word. Examples include the following:

   a. Word: *litter*

   What does the word *litter* mean to a veterinarian, a custodian, and a medic?

   b. Word: *scent*

   What does the word *scent* mean to a chef and a bloodhound?

   c. Word: *crescent*

   What does the word *crescent* mean to a baker, an astronomer, and a mapmaker?

Examples/Nonexamples

1. **Making Choices** encourages students to make choices and justify responses about a word's meaning. Examples include the following:

    a. If any of the following might make someone experience *dread*, say, "dread." Be ready to explain your answer.

    Getting a new puppy

    Hearing a strange noise

    Taking a big test

    Writing a thank you note

    Looking over the edge of a canyon

    b. I'll say some things. If they sound *impudent*, say, "impudent." If they sound *courteous*, say "courteous." Be ready to explain your answer.

    No, thank you.

    That's not the way you pronounce it!

    My mom can cook better than you can.

    May I have some more?

    You didn't give me as much as you gave her!

    c. If any of the things I say might be examples of *philanthropy* say, "philanthropy." If not, don't say anything. Be ready to explain your answer.

    Helping to feed the children of Somalia

    Giving money to your children to help them buy a house

    Helping with a fundraiser to fight breast cancer

    Donating money to a school club in exchange for advertising your company's business

    Donating money to help eradicate malaria and river blindness

    d. If a dog is *timid*, would you pet it or leave it alone? Why?

    e. Is *forage* something your brother would do or something your rabbit would do? Why?

    f. If you had a *sufficient* number of cards, would your deck be complete? Why? Why not?

    g. What would make you feel *indignant*, being chosen for the neighborhood baseball team or being left off of the invitation list for a birthday party? Why?

2. **Child-Created Examples** requires students to create examples that demonstrate their thinking about how the word relates to their background knowledge and life experiences. Examples include the following:

   a.   If your parents set up *consequences* for your poor behavior, what might they be?

   b.   If your sister persisted in *embarrassing* you in front of your friends, how would you respond?

3. **Facets of Word Meaning** stimulates a discussion among students about the critical features of a word's meaning. In this activity, students choose and justify the example that illustrates a word's connotation. Examples include the following:

   a.   Word: *persist*

   During a car trip, a child asks every mile, "Are we there yet?"

   At a rest stop, a child asks for a soda.

   b.   Word: *verify*

   You need to complete any assignments missed during absences.

   You need to bring a note from your parents when you are absent.

   c.   Word: *commitment*

   The skater continued with her lessons, practicing five days a week for several hours each day, until the time of the competition.

   Sam practices his trumpet every chance he gets, but his schedule is quite hectic so he rarely gets to it every day.

   d.   Word: *vicariously*

   The mother felt as if she, rather than her daughter, was having an operation to repair her broken arm.

   The mother sat in the operating room worried as she awaited the results of her daughter's surgery.

Relationships Among Words

Using All of the Words

It is important to develop practice items that include all target words from the selection being read. In the following activity under the subtopic Sentences, all of the words can be incorporated into one practice item or sentence; however, often it is difficult to find a relationship among all of the target words that can fit easily into one thought or idea. The activities titled Choices and One Context for All of the Words illustrate how to develop practice items in cases in which all of the target words cannot easily be incorporated into one sentence.

1. **Relating Words** encourages students to explain and justify their responses to questions and choose words that fit the descriptions given in the sentence. Examples include the following:

   a. Using two words

      Would you *dread* something *appetizing*? Why? Why not?

      When does the moon *cease* being *visible*?

      When might you *verify* a *presumption*?

      If you were in *excruciating* pain, would you *wince*? Why? Why not?

   b. Sentences

      Target words from the selection: *waver, contemplating, sufficient, sacrifice, cease*

      Would you *waver* while *contemplating* sharing cookies with your brother if you thought there was not a *sufficient* number, or would you *sacrifice* some cookies to *cease* arguing? Why?

   c. Choices

      Target words from the selection: *timid, compliant, persistent, frail*

      If you do not want to go to a beach party because there are too many new people to meet, are you *frail* or *timid*? Why?

      If a child refuses to put away his things every time his mother asks him, is he *persistent* or *compliant*? Why?

2. **One Context for All of the Words** promotes students' thinking about the relationship among target words in a selection by asking questions that require knowledge of the words. In the following examples, the words *procrastinate, ramifications,* and *justify* are used in the context of situations involving homework.

   a. Why would you *procrastinate* doing your homework?

   b. What would be the *ramifications* of not doing your homework?

   c. How would you *justify* not completing your homework?

Assessment

Assessments are used to measure students' knowledge of words. The most common format is multiple choice. The previously described activities that promote multiple meaningful exposures can also be used as a valid way to assess a student's acquisition of vocabulary. Following are a few more examples:

1. **Describing/Explaining**

   a. Describe how someone behaves that shows he or she is *indignant.*

   b. Tell about a time you were *baffled.*

   c. Explain a situation that might make someone *wince.*

   d. Mom was excited when she realized that not only was her son accepted by one of the most *prestigious* universities in the country, but he had also been given a full scholarship for the entire time he will be attending. Explain why Mom was so elated.

   e. Place the following phrases on the word line from Little Endurance to Great Deal of Endurance and explain your placement. How much endurance does it take to . . .

   be a spectator at a *decathlon?*

   undergo an *appendectomy?*

   tolerate a child who is having a *tantrum?*

   listen to a *tedious* speaker for over an hour?

       Little Endurance .... Great Deal of Endurance

   f. Place the following phrases on the word line from A Little Anxious to Very Anxious and explain your placement. How anxious would you be if . . .

   you were waiting to see if you received the *position* you wanted?

   airport officials just announced that the mechanical *malfunction* was repaired and the flight would be leaving as scheduled?

   the results of the contest were just about to be *conveyed* to the participants?

   your passport was *invalid?*

       A Little Anxious .... Very Anxious

2. **Relationships Among Words**

   What is alike and/or different between these pairs of words? Explain.

   headstrong/persistent

   timid/frail

   dread/dismay

   waver/baffled

CUMULATIVE REVIEW I

3. **Examples/Nonexamples**

Beat the Clock: Give students 90 seconds to complete 14 items. This activity assesses the students' ability to quickly access words' meanings.

a.	*Timid* mice stay out of sight.	True	False
b.	*Impudent* children are welcome everywhere.	True	False
c.	*Persistent* people give up easily.	True	False
d.	Success is a *consequence* of hard work.	True	False
e.	It is impolite to *stare* at people.	True	False
f.	A restaurant has *sufficient* food.	True	False
g.	The moon is never shaped like a *crescent*.	True	False
h.	The black piano keys were *ebony*.	True	False
i.	The garden is *fragrant* in winter.	True	False
j.	The teacher was *indignant* at my *impudence*.	True	False
k.	Edison *persisted* until he created a light bulb.	True	False
l.	The players *disperse* during Hide and Seek.	True	False
m.	The teacher *presumes* we will fail our test.	True	False
n.	Grandpa was *frail* while recovering from surgery.	True	False

REFERENCE

Beck, I.L., McKeown, M.G., & Kucan, L. (2002). *Bringing words to life: Robust vocabulary instruction.* New York: Guilford Press.

Vocabulary Lesson Design Framework

Target word:

Student friendly definition:

Concrete representation:

Examples within context of selection:
(Note: Remember to tell students why these are examples of the target word.)

Concrete representation:

Examples beyond context of selection:
(Note: Remember to tell students why these are examples of the target word.)

Concrete representation:

Nonexamples:
(Note: Remember to tell students why these are not examples of the target word.)

Concrete representation:

Learning How to Improve Vocabulary Instruction Through Teacher Study Groups by Joseph Dimino & Mary Jo Taylor   125
Copyright © 2009 by Paul H. Brookes Publishing Co., Inc. All rights reserved.

Activity 1 to promote word learning

Activity 2 to promote word learning

Learning How to Improve Vocabulary Instruction Through Teacher Study Groups by Joseph Dimino & Mary Jo Taylor
Copyright © 2009 by Paul H. Brookes Publishing Co., Inc. All rights reserved.

Task Analysis

Selecting Words to Teach (Teacher-Selected Words)

Directions: If fewer than five words were targeted for brief and elaborate instruction, choose additional words from the selection. Use the following steps for each additional word to determine if it requires brief or elaborate instruction. Teach no more than 10 words per selection.

1. Does the word belong in the misdirective or nondirective category? If so, proceed to Step 2. This word may be a candidate for the word bank. If not, proceed to the next word. Descriptions of the natural context categories are as follows:

    • Misdirective: The context leads the reader toward the incorrect meaning of the word.

    • Nondirective: The context does not assist the reader in determining the meaning of the target word.

    • Directive: There is enough information to lead the reader to the correct meaning of the word, or the word is explicitly defined or explained in the text.

    • General: The context provides the reader with adequate information to give a general idea of the word's meaning.

2. Is the word critical (i.e., conceptually central) for understanding the selection? If so, proceed to Step 3. If not, proceed to the next word.

3. Next, consider the student factors.

    a. Ask yourself if the students have had sufficient previous experience with or expo-sure to the word.

    b. Ask yourself if the word will be important for students to know 5 years from now.

    c. Write the word in the word bank if you decided that students have not had sufficient previous experience with or exposure to the word and it will be important for students to know 5 years from now. Repeat Steps 1–3 for the remaining words be-fore proceeding to Step 4.

CUMULATIVE REVIEW I

4. Determine whether each word in the word bank is a Tier 1, Tier 2, or Tier 3 word. Enter each word in the appropriate column. Descriptions of the tiers are as follows:

- Tier 1 are the most basic words (e.g., *desk, run, house*). Students rarely need to be taught these words.

- Tier 2 are high frequency words for mature language users and are found across a variety of subject areas (e.g., *adequate, enormous, vociferous, satisfactory*).

- Tier 3 words are used infrequently and are often limited to a specific subject area (e.g., *chlorophyll, archipelago, diode, ventricle*).

5. Circle the Tier 2 words that are most necessary for comprehending the selection. Again, consider factors such as the importance of the word for understanding the selection, students' knowledge of and exposure to the word, the importance for future learning, socioeconomic status (SES), and English language proficiency.

6. Circle the Tier 1 and Tier 3 words that are critical for comprehending the selection.

7. Decide which of the circled words need only brief instruction. Enter those words in the Brief Instruction column.

8. Decide which of the circled words need more elaborate instruction. Enter those words in the Elaborate Instruction column.

Using Context to Determine Word Meanings

FOCUS RESEARCH CONCEPT

- Using Context to Determine Word Meanings

CUMULATIVE REVIEW

- Previously addressed concepts are not reviewed in this session.

SESSION GOALS

1. Learn the three-step instructional sequence for using context to determine word meanings.
2. Plan a lesson using the three-step instructional sequence.

Overview of the Session

This session gives teachers an opportunity to develop lessons using an instructional sequence designed to help students derive word meanings from context. In the first part of the session, you will debrief on the effectiveness of the lessons you designed in Session 6, Cumulative Review I. Next, the session will address teaching students how to make the most of context to determine the meanings of words. You will review individual lessons and other portions of the teacher's edition looking for evidence of an instructional sequence to teach students how to determine meanings of words in context. Finally, you will review a selection looking for words that will not be explicitly taught and have adequate context for the reader to determine their meanings (i.e., words in the general context category). Using the instructional sequence described, you will plan a lesson that teaches students how to determine the meanings of words in context.

Debrief

During the last collaborative planning session, you developed student friendly definitions, examples, nonexamples, concrete representations, and activities that give students opportunities to interact with words. Describe your lesson and how you thought your students responded. Discuss any questions or concerns you may have. If work samples were collected, examine them for strengths and weaknesses. Consider the following questions to guide the discussion:

- Did you find it difficult to develop activities that promote word learning? Why? Why not?

- Describe one activity you taught.

- Did you teach the lesson as planned? If not, describe any adjustments you made and why you made them.

- How did your students respond to the activity?

Discuss the Focus Research Concept

1. Notice that the focus of this session is on using context to determine word meanings.

2. Some students experience difficulties when they try to derive meaning from context. Researchers have found ways to support students in their efforts to uncover the meanings of unfamiliar words. You will learn how to teach students to look for clues to words' meanings by using the surrounding text to help them.

3. Read Worksheet 7A: Using Context to Determine Word Meanings.

4. After you have read the worksheet, review the four categories of natural context in which words are found (i.e., misdirective, nondirective, general, and directive). You can make the most of context when words fall into the general category.

5. Go over the three steps for using context clues to determine word meanings (also described in Worksheet 7A: Using Context to Determine Word Meanings):

   • Read the sentence with the target word, and look for clues to help you figure out the meaning of the word.

   • Read the sentences before and after the sentence with the target word. Look for clues to help you figure out the meaning of the word.

   • When you think you know what the word means, substitute your meaning for the target word in the sentence. If it makes sense, continue reading. If it does not make sense, try the strategy again.

6. Turn to Worksheet 7B: Study Guide: Using Context to Determine Word Meanings. Read the directions and discuss how you would derive the definition for the first word, *canid*. Compare your responses with the answer key for Worksheet 7B: Study Guide: Using Context to Determine Word Meanings (see the appendix at the end of the book). Determine the meaning of the next two words.

7. Discuss the clues you used to derive your definitions for the words *somniloquy* and *nescient*. Compare your responses with the answer key for Worksheet 7B: Study Guide: Using Context to Determine Word Meanings.

8. Turn to Worksheet 7C: Sample Lesson Using the Instructional Sequence. Read the example of how to use the sequence to determine the meaning of the word *ferry*. This example illustrates the way think-alouds are used to model how a word's meaning can be determined using context.

Compare Research with Practice

Preview the Activity

1. The purpose of this activity is to determine if individual lessons and other sections of the teacher's edition contain an instructional sequence similar to the one described in Worksheet 7A: Using Context to Determine Word Meanings.

2. You will begin by looking at the next three selections you will be teaching. Your task will be to determine if there is an instructional sequence similar to the one described in Worksheet 7A: Using Context to Determine Word Meanings.

3. After you review the selections you will be examining other sections of the teacher's edition (e.g., Differentiating Instruction, Enrichment Activities) to determine if they contain an instructional sequence similar to the one described in Worksheet 7A: Using Context to Determine Word Meanings.

Practice the Activity

1.   Look for instructional sequences similar to those described in Worksheet 7A: Using Context to Determine Word Meanings.

2.   Use Worksheet 7D: Task Analysis: Using Context to Determine Word Meanings to guide you through this activity.

Discuss the Activity

Discuss the following:

1.   Describe the evidence of an instructional sequence you found in a lesson and/or other portions of the teacher's edition that increases students' potential for determining the meanings of words through context. Make sure to discuss whether the instructional sequence you found reflects the intent of the instructional sequence described in Worksheet 7A: Using Context to Determine Word Meanings.

2.   Discuss the similarities and differences in the instructional sequences in your reading program compared with the one described in Worksheet 7A: Using Context to Determine Word Meanings. Keep in mind that there are a variety of useful instructional sequences; however, for the collaborative planning portion of this session, you will practice using the instructional sequence described in this session.

Plan Collaboratively

1.   Turn to Worksheet 7E: Instructional Sequence Template: Using Context to Determine Word Meanings.

2.   Develop lessons for the targeted words you will select using Steps 1 and 2 that follow.

Step 1   Review a selection you will be teaching in your core reading program, and look for words that will not be explicitly taught because there is adequate context for the reader to determine its meaning. These are words that belong in the general category of natural context.

Step 2   Develop lessons using the instructional sequence in Worksheet 7E: Instructional Sequence Template: Using Context to Determine Word Meanings to teach your students how context can be used to help them determine the meaning of words. Be sure to model the instructional sequence at least three times before guiding students through this challenging process.

Assignment

Teach students how to determine the meanings of words in context using the lessons you developed.

Using Context to Determine Word Meanings

It is estimated that an average high school graduate knows the meaning of approximately 40,000 words (Nagy & Herman, 1985). In order to achieve this goal, students need to learn more than 2,600 words each year (seven words per day) from 1st to 12th grade. Between 300 and 400 of those words can be explicitly taught each year. You might wonder how students are learning all of those words. Research indicates that students learn the bulk of those 40,000 words through extensive reading. Wide reading at the appropriate level of difficulty ensures that students will encounter a variety of unknown words and experience the multiple encounters they need to learn them.

Because it is impossible for educators to explicitly and effectively teach seven words each day, students need to be able to determine a word's meaning by using other strategies. In addition to using a dictionary or other reference material and analyzing a word's structure (i.e., affixes, base words, and root words), students should be taught how to use context clues to determine the meaning of words. The National Reading Panel report (2000) supported this approach. It stated that a promising practice to help students increase their vocabulary knowledge is instruction that incorporates both explicitly teaching vocabulary and using word learning strategies that teach students how context can be used to accurately infer the words' meaning. Regardless of the purpose for reading—academic or leisure—it is important to teach students a method they can use to help them construct meaning from context.

There are four categories of context in which words appear: misdirective, nondirective, directive, and general. The word learning strategy addressed in this session will focus on words appearing in general contexts as it provides readers with enough information to give them a general idea of the word's meaning. Misdirective contexts lead the reader to an incorrect definition, and nondirective contexts do not contain enough information to help the reader determine the meaning of the target word.

This three-step word learning strategy is used to decipher the meaning of words in general contexts. The purpose of this strategy is to help students derive a broad meaning of a word in order to support their comprehension of the passage.

1. Read the sentence with the target word and look for clues to help you figure out the meaning of the word.

2. Read the sentences before and after the sentence with the target word. Look for clues to help you figure out the meaning of the word.

3. When you think you know what the word means, substitute your meaning for the target word in the sentence. If it makes sense, continue reading. If it doesn't make sense, try the strategy again.

Let's apply the strategy to the following example with the target word *vertiginous*. "Sylvia had been so excited when Ronald asked her to spend a weekend at his mountain retreat in the Alps. She had envisioned lazy days enjoying the scenery and romantic evenings with wine and candlelight. When she realized Ronald expected her to climb the local mountain peak, it was difficult to change her preconception, but she gamely pulled on her hiking boots. Now, as the memory of that vertiginous climb came back, she had to sit down. She could not remember ever feeling such a sickening and whirling sensation. After such an arduous climb, it seemed unfair that looking down at the valley would produce such an unpleasant experience."

1. Read the sentence with the target word, and look for clues to help you figure out the meaning of the word: "Now, as the memory of that vertiginous climb came back, she had to sit down." The sentence containing the target word does not give the reader enough information to determine its general meaning. The target word could mean *unpleasant, upsetting*, or *frightening*. *Vertiginous* could also mean a pleasant and memorable experience: Sylvia sat down because she wanted to reflect and contemplate on the unforgettable vacation she took in the mountains last year.

2. Read the sentences before and after the sentence with the target word. Look for clues to help you figure out the meaning of the word: "When she realized Ronald expected her to climb the local mountain peak, it was difficult to change her preconception, but she gamely pulled on her hiking boots. Now, as the memory of that vertiginous climb came back, she had to sit down. She could not remember ever feeling such a sickening and whirling sensation."

   The sentence before does not give any clues regarding the meaning of the target word. The information in this sentence takes place before the climb occurred. It was hard for Sylvia to change her preconception of the day's activities, but she willingly put on her boots. In the sentence after, the clues *sickening* and *whirling sensation* lead the reader to conclude that *dizzying* is a sensible meaning for *vertiginous*.

3. When you think you know what the word means, substitute your meaning for the target word in the sentence. If it makes sense, continue reading. If it doesn't make sense, try the strategy again: Now, as the memory of that *sickening* climb came back, she had to sit down. Both words make sense in the sentence even though the form of the adjective *dizzy* had to be modified. *Vertiginous* means causing dizziness, especially when one is at a high altitude. The information within the context of the selection gives readers enough information to formulate a definition that maintains their comprehension of the selection.

Scaffolded Instruction

It is important to teach this strategy using the three critical aspects of explicit instruction that include modeling, guided practice, and independent practice. Vygotsky (1978) brought these phases of scaffolded instruction to our attention. The term is linked to his concept of the Zone of Proximal Development (ZPD). According to Vygotsky, the ZPD is the difference between the skills and strategies learners are able to accomplish independently and those

USING CONTEXT TO DETERMINE WORD MEANINGS

7

that are emerging and can be completed with teacher support. The teacher begins by providing a significant amount of support during the modeling phase. As students' proficiency increases, teacher support is systematically released. Consequently, as the process continues, the teacher moves to the guided practice phase in which her role evolves into that of a facilitator until students can complete the task independently and automatically. There is no rule regarding the number of days each phase of scaffolded instruction should last. Moving through the phases depends on the level of difficulty students are experiencing at each phase. This is a professional judgment that is made by monitoring student performance during instruction.

REFERENCES

Nagy, W.E., & Herman, P.A. (1985). Incidental vs. instructional approaches to increasing reading vocabulary. *Educational Perspectives, 1,* 16–21.

National Reading Panel. (2000). *Report of the National Reading Panel: Teaching children to read: An evidence-based assessment of the scientific research literature on reading and its implications for reading instruction.* Washington, DC: National Institute of Child Health and Human Development.

Vygotsky, L.S. (1978). *Mind in society: The development of higher psychological processes.* (M. Cole, V. John-Steiner, S. Scribner, & E. Souberman, Eds. & Trans.). Cambridge, MA: Harvard University Press.

Study Guide

Using Context to Determine Word Meanings

Directions: Read each paragraph and determine the meaning of the italicized target word by using the steps of the word learning strategy. Write your definition in the space provided. Indicate which sentence(s) contain the clues that helped you develop your definition (e.g., the sentence containing the target word; the sentence before, and the sentence after).

1. Read the sentence with the target word, and look for clues to help you figure out the meaning of the word.

2. Read the sentences before and after the sentence with the target word. Look for clues to help you figure out the meaning of the word.

3. When you think you know what the word means, substitute your meaning for the target word in the sentence. If it makes sense, continue reading. If it doesn't make sense, try the strategy again.

Our friend, a famous wildlife artist, had a rather intense interest in wolves, dogs, foxes, and similar four-legged animals. His studio always had at least a few residents, sometimes a Chihuahua, at other times a wolfish-looking shepherd mix. We were always a little nervous around the *canid* skulls on his window ledge. It would be impolite to ask him whether they were fossils for artistic inspiration or mementos of his past companions.

Definition: _____

_____

In which sentence(s) did you find the clues? _____

_____

_____

_____

_____

_____

Explain how the clues helped you figure out the definition. _____

_____

_____

_____

_____

_____

Sarah was having more and more difficulty staying awake through the interminable lectures in the science hall. When she could not read her notes for the upcoming final exam, she went into her study and made the call. Later that evening, she approached her husband with the news: "Clarence, I have made an appointment for you with a doctor who specializes in *somniloquy.* I want you to go because the sounds you are making when you sleep keep me awake at night and it is affecting my grades."

Definition: _____

_____

In which sentence(s) did you find the clues? _____

_____

_____

_____

_____

_____

Explain how the clues helped you figure out the definition. _____

_____

_____

_____

_____

Tabloid papers available at every supermarket checkout line scream insane headlines: "Civil War Baby Found at Battlefield," "Ninety-year-old Woman Pregnant with Triplets!" Editors must think that the people who read their publication are unaware, oblivious, unintelligent, and not very well informed, sharing a common assertion that individuals who read tabloids are *nescient* readers. I can only hope people who buy these publications at least try to verify some of the printed information.

Definition: _____

_____

In which sentence(s) did you find the clues? _____

_____

_____

_____

_____

_____

Explain how the clues helped you figure out the definition. _____

_____

_____

_____

_____

**WORKSHEET
7C**

Sample Lesson Using the Instructional Sequence

Note: This is an example of a lesson that models how to teach students to determine the meaning of words in context using the instructional sequence described.

Selection: A Special Visit

Target Word: _____*ferry*_____

I live on Whidbey Island in the State of Washington. Every Sunday, my family and I visit my grandmother. The five of us pile into my dad's car and drive to the waterfront where there are many boats in the water. Dad drives our car onto a ferry. The ferry takes us across the beautiful blue water of the Puget Sound to Seattle. We always have a good time when we visit our grandmother.

1. Read the sentence with the target word and look for clues to help you figure out the meaning of the word.

   a. Dad drives our car onto a ferry.

   b. Think-aloud: The sentence with the word *ferry* does not give us clues about the word's meaning. In this sentence, *ferry* could mean that dad drives the car onto a tow truck or bridge.

2. Read the sentences before and after the sentence with the target word. Look for clues to help figure out the meaning of the word.

   a. Sentence before: "The five of us pile into my dad's car and drive to the waterfront where there are many boats in the water."

   b. Sentence after: "The ferry takes us across the beautiful blue water of the Puget Sound to Seattle."

   c. Think-aloud: The sentence before does not give clues about the word's meaning. The sentence after states that the ferry takes us across the water. Something that takes you across the water could be a boat. *Ferry* could mean *boat*.

3. When you think you know what the word means, substitute your meaning for the target word in the sentence. If it makes sense, continue reading. If it doesn't make sense, try the strategy again.

   a. Think-aloud: Change the word *ferry* to *boat* and see if the sentence makes sense. The boat takes us across the beautiful blue water of the Puget Sound to Seattle. Because it makes sense, *boat* is a good definition for *ferry*.

**WORKSHEET
7D**

Task Analysis

Using Context to Determine Word Meanings

7

Directions: Use the following steps to determine if your core program contains an instructional sequence to help students determine the meaning of words through context.

1. Review the next three selections you are going to be teaching, and look for an instructional sequence to help students determine the meaning of words in context. If a strategy is present, write the page number in the following table.

2. After reviewing the selections, examine other sections of the teacher's edition (e.g., Differentiating Instruction, Enrichment Activities) to determine if they contain an instructional sequence similar to the one described in Worksheet 7A: Using Context to Determine Word Meanings. If so, enter the page number in the following table.

Making the Most of Natural Contexts Table

Page number	Page number	Page number
Page number	Page number	Page number
Page number	Page number	Page number

Instructional Sequence Template

Using Context to Determine Word Meanings

Directions: Complete this instructional sequence to model how to determine a word's meaning through context.

Target Word: _____

1. Read the sentence with the target word and look for clues to help you figure out the meaning of the word.

   Think-aloud: _____

   _____

   _____

   _____

   _____

   _____

2. Read the sentences before and after the sentence with the target word. Look for clues to help you figure out the meaning of the word.

   Think-aloud: _____

   _____

   _____

   _____

   _____

   _____

3. When you think you know what the word means, substitute your meaning for the target word in the sentence. If it makes sense, continue reading. If it doesn't make sense, try the strategy again.

   Think-aloud: _____

   _____

   _____

   _____

   _____

   _____

Reviewing and Extending Word Learning

FOCUS RESEARCH CONCEPT

• Developing Cumulative Review and Extension Activities

CUMULATIVE REVIEW

• Previously addressed concepts are not reviewed in this session.

SESSION GOALS

1. Learn activities that provide students with a cumulative review of previously learned words within and beyond the classroom.
2. Learn activities that raise students' curiosity about and awareness of words in their environment within and beyond the classroom.
3. Develop a plan for implementing activities and procedures to cumulatively review previously taught words and raise students' awareness of and interest in words they encounter in their environment.

8

Overview of the Session

Teachers can use a variety of activities and procedures to help students acquire a deep understanding of previously taught vocabulary and a desire to learn about new words they encounter in their environment. This session gives you the opportunity to study, develop, and implement activities and procedures that extend word learning. These activities are intended to enhance students' understanding of previously taught words and raise their awareness of and curiosity about words in their environment.

In the first part of the session, you will debrief the lessons you developed using the instructional sequence presented in the last session. Then you will review Worksheet 8A: Activities to Review and Extend Word Learning. Next, you will focus on extension activities students can engage in both within and beyond the classroom to reinforce previously learned words and to raise their awareness of words in their environment. You will also review individual lessons and other portions of the teacher's edition looking for evidence of the type of activities and procedures similar to those described in Worksheet 8A: Activities to Review and Extend Word Learning. You will then develop a plan for implementing activities that reinforce previously learned vocabulary and build awareness of and interest in new words.

Debrief

Debrief the lessons you taught using the instructional sequence presented in Session 7. Consider the following to guide the discussion:

- Describe your experience developing lessons based on the instructional sequence presented in Session 7.

- Describe a lesson you taught.

- Did you teach the lesson as planned? If not, describe any adjustments you made and why you made them.

Discuss the Focus Research Concept

1. Notice the topic of this session, Reviewing and Extending Word Learning. You will be learning about activities and procedures you can use both within and beyond the classroom to cumulatively review previously learned words and raise students' awareness of words in the environment.

2. Read Worksheet 8A: Activities to Review and Extend Word Learning.

3. Discuss the activities in Worksheet 8A: Activities to Review and Extend Word Learning using the following procedure. Make four columns labeled Cumulative Review: Within the Classroom, Cumulative Review: Beyond the

Classroom, Raising Students' Awareness of and Curiosity About Words: Within the Classroom, and Raising Students' Awareness of and Curiosity About Words: Beyond the Classroom. Respond to the following questions and write your responses in the appropriate column. Refer to Worksheet 8A: Activities to Review and Extend Word Learning for ideas. You will be using some of the activities from all four categories for this session's collaborative planning.

   a. What ideas are recommended for cumulative review within the classroom to reinforce the learning of words presented in the lesson?

   b. How can teachers promote cumulative review beyond the classroom?

   c. What are some activities teachers can use to raise students' awareness of and interest in words within the classroom?

   d. Name some activities teachers can use to raise awareness of and interest in words beyond the classroom.

   e. Are there other activities you use for cumulative review or raising students' awareness of words that were not mentioned?

4. Turn to Worksheet 8B: Additional Activities to Review and Extend Word Learning. You will be referring to these activities during the collaborative planning portion of this session.

Compare Research with Practice

Preview the Activity

1. The purpose of this activity is to determine if the individual lessons and other sections of the teacher's edition contain activities similar to those described in the Cumulative Review and Raising Students' Awareness of and Curiosity About Words sections of Worksheet 8A: Activities to Review and Extend Word Learning.

2. You will begin by looking at the next three selections you will be teaching to determine if there are any activities that are similar to those identified in the Cumulative Review section of Worksheet 8A: Activities to Review and Extend Word Learning.

3. You will then examine the same three selections for evidence of any activities that are similar to the Raising Students' Awareness of and Curiosity About Words section of Worksheet 8A: Activities to Review and Extend Word Learning.

4. Next, after reviewing the selections, you will be examining other sections of the teacher's edition (e.g., Differentiating Instruction, Enrichment Activities) to determine if they contain activities similar to those identified in the Cumulative Review section in Worksheet 8A: Activities to Review and Extend Word Learning.

5. Finally, after reviewing the selections, you will be examining other sections of the teacher's edition (e.g., Differentiating Instruction, Enrichment Activities) to determine if they contain activities similar to those identified in the Raising Students' Awareness of and Curiosity About Words section in Worksheet 8A: Activities to Review and Extend Word Learning.

Practice the Activity

1. Turn to Worksheet 8D: Evidence of Activities to Review and Extend Word Learning Table.

2. Use Worksheet 8C: Task Analysis: Evidence of Activities to Review and Extend Word Learning to guide you through the activity.

Discuss the Activity

Discuss the following when you have finished this activity. Make sure to consider whether the activities and procedures you found reflect the intent of those described in the Cumulative Review and Raising Students' Awareness of and Curiosity About Words sections of Worksheet 8A: Activities to Review and Extend Word Learning.

1. Describe the activities you found that help students acquire a deep understanding of previously taught vocabulary in the Cumulative Review category.

2. Describe the activities you found in the category Raising Students' Awareness of and Curiosity About Words.

Plan Collaboratively

1. Turn to Worksheet 8E (1–4): Implementation Plan.

2. Use Steps 3–8 below to adapt or create an activity for each of the following categories:

    a. Cumulative Review Activities (Within the Classroom)

    b. Cumulative Review Activities (Beyond the Classroom)

    c. Raising Students' Awareness of and Curiosity About Words (Within the Classroom)

    d. Raising Students' Awareness of and Curiosity About Words (Beyond the Classroom)

3. Decide whether you will work individually, with partners, in small groups, or in grade-level teams.

4. Choose a recorder for the group.

5. Choose a reporter.

6. Develop activities similar to those described in Worksheet 8A: Activities to Review and Extend Word Learning by:

   a. Adapting one of the activities or procedures described in Worksheet 8A: Activities to Review and Extend Word Learning and/or Worksheet 8B: Additional Activities to Review and Extend Word Learning so that it fits closely with the intent of Reviewing and Extending Word Learning and can be easily implemented into your classroom routine.

   OR

   b. Creating a fresh idea for an activity that is similar in nature to those ideas described in Worksheet 8A: Activities to Review and Extend Word Learning and/or Worksheet 8B: Additional Activities to Review and Extend Word Learning.

7. Using Worksheet 8E (1 and 2): Implementation Plan, develop the materials you will need for each of the activities you adapted or developed for the two categories of Cumulative Review Activities (Within the Classroom) and Cumulative Review Activities (Beyond the Classroom).

8. Using Worksheet 8E (3 and 4): Implementation Plan, develop the materials you will need for each of the activities you adapted or developed for the two categories of Raising Students' Awareness of and Curiosity About Words (Within the Classroom) and Raising Students' Awareness of and Curiosity About Words (Beyond the Classroom).

9. Share the activity you adapted or created.

Assignment

Implement the activities to enhance vocabulary learning.

Activities to Review and Extend Word Learning

Session 5 was devoted to identifying several types of engaging activities that give students multiple exposures to new words. These interactive experiences are used after the teacher has provided a thorough explanation of a word to help students internalize its meaning. Though vitally important, these activities are not enough. Effective vocabulary instruction should also include two additional goals: 1) cumulatively reviewing previously learned words, and 2) raising students' awareness of and curiosity about words. To achieve these goals, teachers should design activities within and beyond the classroom.

Cumulative Review

Cumulatively reviewing previously learned vocabulary within the classroom can be accomplished through whole-class and independent activities. An ideal way is to have students actively participate in adapted versions of games such as musical chairs, Tic-Tac-Toe, relay races, and charades. Another is to create learning centers in which students can work independently. Engaging activities like word puzzles, word games, or those similar to the ones described in Session 5 can be used. Worksheets can be appropriate, especially if they include exercises that foster deeper understanding of words by requiring students to develop analogies, metaphors, detailed descriptions, examples, and nonexamples. Use activities similar to those addressed in Session 5 to develop worksheets that enhance word learning.

Supporting students' vocabulary learning beyond the classroom can be accomplished using resources in the school and involving parents at home. Both involve creating a plan that will give students ample practice with the words they have learned. These can be both fun and meaningful. One example is the Word Wizard activity described by Beck, McKeown, and Kucan (2002). In this activity, students went through the school carrying index cards with previously learned words written on them. Any adult could read the word on one of the cards and ask the child to explain its meaning.

In another activity, a teacher arranged for her students to dress up as a word they had previously learned and parade around the school. Students portrayed such words as *glitter* and *inflame*. One student taped dollar bills to herself to exemplify the word *wealth*. Music, art, and physical education teachers can also help reinforce vocabulary by integrating words into their lessons.

At home, parents can use the targeted vocabulary in conversations with their children. They can help their children use words in creative stories, homework assignments, or letters or e-mails to relatives and friends.

Raising Students' Awareness of and Curiosity About Words

Even though teachers determine most of the words they want students to learn, they can also help students become more aware of interesting and intriguing words in their environment. Within the classroom, teachers can ask students to write down interesting words they hear throughout the day. One group of teachers introduced the word jar concept by reading *Donavan's Word Jar* by Monalisa De Gross (1994). Students placed words on a poster of a large jar like Donavan's when they heard them in daily conversations or while reading. Three times a week, the teacher selected one or two words. She pronounced each word and provided a student friendly definition, examples, and nonexamples. Students were encouraged to use these words during discussions, conversations, and writing. The teacher periodically reviewed the words and placed a sticker, star, or checkmark beside them once they became part of the class' vocabulary.

Finding interesting words beyond the classroom can include those heard during school assemblies, field trips, guest speakers' visits, special event days, or Word of the Day programs. At home, students can acquire many words from their conversations with adults and from the books that are read aloud to them. Students' vocabularies are also expanded when parents take their children to a movie, a zoo, a museum, a shopping center, or to a family function. Parents can be encouraged to help their children listen for interesting words as they play board games, cook supper, or clean the house together. Comic books, newspapers, magazines, and television programs are good, readily available resources for students to discover interesting words.

REFERENCES

Beck, I.L., McKeown, M.G., & Kucan, L. (2002). *Bringing words to life: Robust vocabulary instruction*. New York: Guilford Press.

DeGross, M. (1994). *Donavan's word jar*. New York: HarperCollins.

WORKSHEET 8B

Additional Activities to Review and Extend Word Learning

Cumulative Review (Within the Classroom)

Human Tic-Tac-Toe

Nine chairs are arranged in three rows. Students are divided into two teams: *X* and *O*. The teams line up on opposite sides of chairs and several feet away. The teacher selects a word from a list or from cards, and the first player must perform the assigned task (e.g., define the word, use it in a meaningful sentence, give an example or a nonexample). If the player correctly performs the task, she sits in whichever chair the team believes is most strategic. If she is an *X*, her arms will be crossed across her chest. If she is an *O*, her hands will form a circle. Play continues from one team to another, and players take a seat to complete the lines of *X* or *O* just as in the paper version: across, down, or diagonally. The first team to finish a line wins.

Materials:

- A list of words
- A menu of vocabulary tasks

Musical Chairs

Chairs are arranged so that there is one fewer than the number of students. Students line up around the chairs and begin to move when the teacher (or leader) begins playing music. When the teacher stops the music, students find a chair and sit. One student will be left without a chair. At this point, the teacher asks the student who is without a chair to choose a seated player. The teacher asks the seated player to perform a vocabulary task (e.g., define the word, use it in a meaningful sentence, give an example). If the seated player cannot perform the task, the student without a chair replaces him in the seat. A chair is removed and play continues until there is only one player left.

Materials:

- A list of words
- A menu of vocabulary tasks

Charades

Students are divided into four or five groups. The teacher chooses a word and tells one of the students in a group to take 30 seconds to think about how to act out the word for the team. After 30 seconds, the student has 2 minutes to act out the word while his teammates are shouting out guesses. If his team does not guess the word correctly within 2 minutes, the teacher gives that card to a person in the next group who will act it out for her team. Teams earn one point for every word that is correctly identified.

Materials:

- A list of words
- Score card
- Timer

Twenty Questions

Students are placed into groups. The teacher secretly selects a word from a set of five previously taught words that she has listed on the board. Each group may ask the teacher one question that will help it determine the word. Only *yes* or *no* questions can be asked. Group members work together to determine the question. One student is designated to ask the question. There should be a time limit for developing each question. Using a timekeeper is good for keeping groups on task. If students do not determine the word within the 20-question limit, the teacher reveals the word.

Materials:

- A list of words
- Timer

Progressive Story

Students are placed into groups of four or five. The teacher selects a word from a list of previously taught vocabulary. She writes the first part of the story using a word or words from the list. The story passes to the first group who selects the next word or words and continues the story. The story passes to all groups, with the last group using its word or words to end the story. A scribe should be designated for each group.

Materials:

- A list of words
- Beginning sentence(s)

Baseball

The class is divided into two teams. A baseball diamond is drawn on the board. Play progresses in the same manner as an actual baseball game, except that each player must perform a vocabulary task in order to advance to the next base. If the player wishes to hit a home run, she will need to perform a more difficult task. It is up to the teacher to decide whether a player may conference with her teammates in order to perform the required task.

Materials:

- A list of words
- A menu of vocabulary tasks (easy and more difficult)

Affinity Diagram

The teacher writes words on index cards that students have learned over the course of a week and places them on the classroom bulletin board. At the end of each week, groups of students take turns sorting the cards into like categories. Word cards can be moved among categories any number of times. Grouping is finished when most of the members of each group are no longer moving cards from category to category. After all of the groups have taken a turn, the teacher views the display and discusses the words and their categories with the class.

Materials:

- Letter to staff explaining how to conduct the activity
- Index cards

REVIEWING AND EXTENDING WORD LEARNING

Cumulative Review (Beyond the Classroom)

Concentration (Pairs)

This activity can be completed in school, during lunch, at indoor recess, in after-school care, or at home with parents. The teacher prepares a set of cards made up of pairs with the target word on one card and a definition, an example, or a nonexample on the other. The cards are placed face down. The first player turns over two cards. If they match, she keeps the set. If not, the cards are turned over. The player who collects the most pairs wins.

   Materials:

   • A list of words

   • Definitions, examples, and nonexamples

   • Letter to staff and/or parents explaining how to conduct the activity

Create a Story or a Poem (Individual)

This activity can be completed in school, during lunch, at indoor recess, in after-school care, or at home. The teacher provides a list of previously taught words. Students select words and use them meaningfully in a story or poem.

   Materials:

   • A list of words

   • Letter to school staff and/or parents explaining how to conduct the activity

Playing Board Games

This activity can be completed in school, during lunch, at indoor recess, in after-school care, or at home. Store-bought games can be used to reinforce vocabulary words. In order to advance, children have to define a word they learned, use it in a meaningful sentence, or give an example or nonexample. Use this activity with simple games (e.g., Candy Land, Chutes and Ladders, Life, Parcheesi).

   Materials:

   • A list of words

   • A menu of vocabulary tasks

   • Letter to staff and/or parents explaining how to conduct the activity

Vocabulary in a Flash

This activity can be completed in school, during lunch, at indoor recess, in after-school care, or at home. The teacher creates a list of previously taught words and their student friendly definitions or examples. The teacher writes a word on one side of the index card and the definition or an example on the other side. The adult who is conducting the activity begins by selecting three of the words and reviewing their pronunciations, definitions, or examples. Once the words have been reviewed, a student is presented with a set of flash cards. It is the student's turn to pronounce the word and give its definition or an example. Once the student is able to say the word, state its definition, or give an example at least three rounds, the adult drops that word and adds an unfamiliar word to the pile.

Materials:

- A set of cards with the word on one side and the definition or example on the opposite side

- Letter to staff and/or parents explaining how to conduct the activity

Raising Students' Awareness of and Curiosity About Words (Within the Classroom)

Hidden Words

The teacher intentionally places unfamiliar words around the classroom (e.g., at learning centers, on bulletin boards) or mentions words she thinks students do not know. When students notice the teacher using these unfamiliar words, they are instructed to call her attention to them. When they do, the teacher writes the words on a chart and gives a brief, student friendly definition. She should consciously attempt to use them during the day. Each time she does and the students notice, a checkmark is placed next to the word on the chart.

Materials:

- A list of unfamiliar words

- A word chart

Design Day

Throughout the week, students collect words they find interesting in the classroom. The teacher chooses three or four of them and provides students with a student friendly definition, an example, and a nonexample. Students work in groups to demonstrate understanding of one of the words. They can design a pennant or decorate the classroom door or can write on an old T-shirt, bag, or box. Student products must include a student friendly definition, a concrete representation, an example, and a nonexample for their word.

Materials:

- A list of supplies for completing the activity

Comic Books

The teacher divides students into groups of four or five. Each group is asked to locate an interesting word in a comic book. The students are to cut out the words in context with the accompanying illustration. The group members work together to determine the word's meaning. The teacher monitors and assists students as they complete the activity. At the end of class, the teacher calls on a few groups to identify their word and tell what it means. He elaborates by extending and clarifying the definition and providing examples.

Materials:

- Comic books

- A list of potential words generated from a prior review of the comic books

8

Daily Message

Each day the teacher can write a message on the board containing a word that is unfamiliar and that many students would find interesting. The teacher discusses the word during the morning message and uses it many times throughout the day.

Materials:

- A few morning messages

Class Dictionary

The teacher picks a new or unusual word that begins with the letter *A*. She writes the word on the front of an index card. On the back, the teacher writes a student friendly definition, an example, and a nonexample. After explaining the word, the teacher asks students to draw a picture illustrating the word. For example, to illustrate the word *appreciation*, a student draws a picture of himself smiling as his parents give him a toy. On another day, the teacher moves to the letter *B*. Over time, each student will have a class dictionary.

Materials:

- List of words for each letter of the alphabet

- Definitions, examples, and nonexamples

Raising Students' Awareness of and Curiosity About Words (Beyond the Classroom)

Scrapbook

While looking through old scrapbooks and/or family pictures, parents can share interesting words that describe the pictures and/or relate to the family event that took place. Students can then write these words in a scrapbook of interesting words of their own.

Materials:

- Letter to parents explaining the activity

Going Places

While running errands to the post office, dry cleaners, or grocery store, parents can give their child several explanations about what is going on (e.g., "The scanner we use at the checkout counter in the grocery store tells us the cost of the items we purchased; *purchased* means to buy," "The cost of the items we purchased is *exorbitant*" [the parent then explains *exorbitant*]).

Materials:

- Letter to parents explaining how to conduct the activity

Reading Aloud

The teacher reminds parents that reading aloud to their children is important and should continue long after they have begun to read independently. Children's listening comprehension is often higher than the level at which they can read. Parents are asked to highlight vocabulary words in a reading that they think may be difficult for their child to understand. Next parents should talk about the word and tell their child what it means in child friendly language. Parents can provide a couple of examples to clarify the word's meaning, then find ways to use those words repeatedly in daily conversation with the child. Parents are asked to consider keeping a journal to record those words.

Materials:

- Letter to parents explaining how to conduct the activity

Describing Objects

Parents can ask their child to point out an object in the house. The child and parents then take turns coming up with adjectives that describe the object. They see how many of the words they can think of to describe the object. For example, an orange might be described as a large orange; a large, round orange; a large, round, juicy orange; a large, round, juicy, scrumptious orange; or a large, round, juicy, scrumptious, delectable orange. The goal is to keep describing the object using as many adjectives as possible. This approach is attempted with another object.

Materials:

- Letter to parents explaining how to conduct the activity

Task Analysis

Evidence of Activities to Review and Extend Word Learning

Directions: Use the following steps to determine if your core reading program contains activities similar to those described in the Cumulative Review and Raising Students' Awareness of and Curiosity About Words sections from Worksheet 8A: Activities to Review and Extend Word Learning.

1. Review individual lessons and look for activities similar to those in the Cumulative Review and Raising Students' Awareness of and Curiosity About Words sections from Worksheet 8A: Activities to Review and Extend Word Learning. If procedures are present, enter the page number and the name of the activity in the appropriate column on the table provided in Worksheet 8D: Evidence of Activities to Review and Extend Word Learning Table.

2. Review other portions of the teacher's edition to determine if there are activities similar to those identified in the Cumulative Review and Raising Students' Awareness of and Curiosity About Words sections from Worksheet 8A: Activities to Review and Extend Word Learning. These sections often are entitled Differentiating Instruction, Enrichment Activities, and so forth. If activities are present, write the page number and the name of the activity in the appropriate columns on the table provided in Worksheet 8D: Evidence of Activities to Review and Extend Word Learning Table.

Evidence of Activities to Review and Extend Word Learning Table

Cumulative Review

Within the classroom evidence (page number)	Name of the activity
Beyond the classroom evidence (page number)	**Name of the activity**

Raising Students' Awareness of and Curiosity About Words

Within the classroom evidence (page number)	Name of the activity
Beyond the classroom evidence (page number)	**Name of the activity**

**WORKSHEET
8E (1)**

Implementation Plan

*Cumulative Review Activities
(Within the Classroom)*

Directions: Prepare the materials that are needed for the activity you adapted or developed. Only complete the sets of materials applicable for this activity.

Title of the activity: _____

Set 1 materials:

- Include a list of words and student friendly definitions, examples, nonexamples, and so forth.

_____

_____

_____

_____

Set 2 materials:

- Compose a letter to staff and/or parents that will explain how to conduct the activity.

_____

_____

_____

_____

Set 3 materials:

- Include additional materials you will need to conduct the activity (e.g., game pieces, puzzles, morning messages).

_____

_____

_____

_____

Copyright © 2009 by Paul H. Brookes Publishing Co., Inc. All rights reserved.

Implementation Plan

Cumulative Review Activities (Beyond the Classroom)

Directions: Prepare the materials that are needed for the activity you adapted or developed. Only complete the sets of materials applicable for this activity.

Title of the activity: _____

Set 1 materials:

- Include a list of words and student friendly definitions, examples, nonexamples, and so forth.

_____

_____

_____

_____

Set 2 materials:

- Compose a letter to staff and/or parents that will explain how to conduct the activity.

_____

_____

_____

_____

Set 3 materials:

- Include additional materials you will need to conduct the activity (e.g., game pieces, puzzles, morning messages).

_____

_____

_____

_____

Copyright © 2009 by Paul H. Brookes Publishing Co., Inc. All rights reserved

Implementation Plan

Raising Students' Awareness of and Curiosity About Words (Within the Classroom)

Directions: Prepare the materials that are needed for the activity you adapted or developed. Only complete the sets of materials applicable for this activity.

Title of the activity: _____

Set 1 materials:

- Include a list of words and student friendly definitions, examples, nonexamples, and so forth.

_____

_____

_____

_____

Set 2 materials:

- Compose a letter to staff and/or parents that will explain how to conduct the activity.

_____

_____

_____

_____

Set 3 materials:

- Include additional materials you will need to conduct the activity (e.g., game pieces, puzzles, morning messages).

_____

_____

_____

_____

Copyright © 2009 by Paul H. Brookes Publishing Co., Inc. All rights reserved.

Implementation Plan

Raising Students' Awareness of and Curiosity About Words (Beyond the Classroom)

Directions: Prepare the materials that are needed for the activity you adapted or developed. Only complete the sets of materials applicable for this activity.

Title of the activity: _____

Set 1 materials:

- Include a list of words and student friendly definitions, examples, nonexamples, and so forth.

_____

_____

_____

_____

Set 2 materials:

- Compose a letter to staff and/or parents that will explain how to conduct the activity.

_____

_____

_____

_____

Set 3 materials:

- Include additional materials you will need to conduct the activity (e.g., game pieces, puzzles, morning messages).

_____

_____

_____

_____

Copyright © 2009 by Paul H. Brookes Publishing Co., Inc. All rights reserved.

VOCABULARY SESSION

Cumulative Review II

CUMULATIVE REVIEW

- Categories of Natural Context: Misdirective, Nondirective, Directive, and General
- Selecting Words to Teach
- Developing Student Friendly Definitions
- Developing Examples, Nonexamples, and Concrete Representations
- Developing Activities to Promote Word Learning

SESSION GOALS

1. Plan a lesson that includes student friendly definitions, examples, nonexamples, and activities that allow students to interact with words.

Overview of the Session

This session will serve as a cumulative review of the major research concepts addressed in Sessions 2–5. The activities you will complete are the same as those in Session 6, Cumulative Review I. They include determining which of the publisher's recommended words require brief or elaborate instruction followed by activities to determine if those targeted words include student friendly definitions, examples, nonexamples, concrete representations, and activities that promote word learning. You will also develop a vocabulary lesson that incorporates these components.

Debrief

During the last collaborative planning session, you developed activities to review and extend word learning. Describe your activity and discuss how your students responded. Provide feedback to your colleagues by responding to their questions and concerns. If student work was collected, examine it for strengths and weaknesses. Consider the following to guide the discussion.

- Describe the activities you implemented in your classroom.

- How did your students respond to the activity?

- How will you embed these activities into your classroom routine?

Review the Focus Research Concept

The purpose of this session is to review and practice applying the research concepts presented in the previous sessions; therefore, no new research will be discussed.

Compare Research with Practice

Preview the Activity

1. The purpose of this activity is to provide a review and additional practice applying the research concepts presented in Sessions 2–5. You will put it all together by determining which of the publisher's recommended words will require brief or elaborate instruction followed by activities to determine which of these words include student friendly definitions, examples, nonexamples, concrete representations, and/or activities that promote word learning.

2. You will need the following worksheets for these activities:

   - Worksheet 9A: Task Analysis: Selecting Words to Teach (Words Recommended by the Publisher)

   - Worksheet 9B: Selecting Words to Teach Table

   - Worksheet 9C: Task Analysis: Student Friendly/Not Student Friendly, Examples, Nonexamples, Concrete Representations, and Activities to Promote Word Learning

   - Worksheet 9D: Student Friendly/Not Student Friendly, Examples, Nonexamples, Concrete Representations, Activity Table

Practice the Activity

1. Turn to Worksheet 9A: Task Analysis: Selecting Words to Teach (Words Recommended by the Publisher) and Worksheet 9B: Selecting Words to Teach Table. A task analysis is provided to guide you in selecting words to teach.

2. Turn to Worksheet 9C: Task Analysis: Student Friendly/Not Student Friendly, Examples, Nonexamples, Concrete Representations, and Activities to Promote Word Learning and Worksheet 9D: Student Friendly/Not Student Friendly, Examples, Nonexamples, Concrete Representations, Activity Table. Use the task analysis to sort the words you selected for brief or elaborate instruction into the Student Friendly/Not Friendly categories, and determine whether the publisher's instructional recommendations include examples, nonexamples, concrete representations, and activities that promote word learning.

Discuss the Activity

Discuss the following questions:

a. What evidence was there of student friendly definitions, examples, nonexamples, and concrete recommendations?

b. Did you find evidence of activities that allow students to interact with words? Describe them.

Plan Collaboratively

1. You will develop student friendly definitions, examples, nonexamples, and concrete representations for the words you analyzed in the Practice the Activity portion of this session. You will also develop activities that give students opportunities to interact with these words. A task analysis is provided to guide you through this activity (see Worksheet 9E: Examples of Activities to Promote Word Learning).

2. Turn to Worksheet 9F: Vocabulary Lesson Design Framework. Complete one Worksheet 9F: Vocabulary Lesson Design Framework for each word in the Brief and Elaborate Instruction columns.

3. Develop student friendly definitions for the words you wrote in the Not Student Friendly column of Worksheet 9D: Student Friendly/Not Student Friendly, Examples, Nonexamples, Concrete Representations, Activity Table. Write the definitions in the Student Friendly Definition section of Worksheet 9F: Vocabulary Lesson Design Framework.

4. For some of the defined words, there will be no evidence of examples, nonexamples, concrete representations, and activities that promote word learning. Develop student friendly definitions, examples, nonexamples, and concrete representation for the words you wrote in the Brief and Elaborate Instruction columns. Develop activities for the words you wrote in the Elaborate Instruction column. Write this information in the corresponding sections of Worksheet 9F: Vocabulary Lesson Design Framework.

5. If fewer than five words were targeted for brief and elaborate instruction, choose additional words from the selection by completing the Selecting Words to Teach activity using Worksheet 9G: Task Analysis: Selecting Words to Teach (Teacher-Selected Words). Add these words to Worksheet 9B: Selecting Words to Teach Table. Teach no more than 10 words per selection.

6. Develop student friendly definitions, examples, nonexamples, and concrete representations for the additional words you wrote in the Brief and Elaborate Instruction columns of Worksheet 9B: Selecting Words to Teach Table. Write this information in the corresponding sections of Worksheet 9F: Vocabulary Lesson Design Framework. Keep in mind that some words may not lend themselves to concrete representations.

7. Develop activities for the words you wrote in the Elaborate Instruction column of Worksheet 9B: Selecting Words to Teach Table. Write this information in the appropriate sections of Worksheet 9F: Vocabulary Lesson Design Framework.

Assignment

Teach the vocabulary using student friendly definitions, examples, nonexamples, concrete representations, and the activities you developed.

WORKSHEET 9A

Task Analysis

Selecting Words to Teach (Words Recommended by the Publisher)

9

Directions: Choose a selection in the core reading program. Review the words the publisher recommends teaching students before they read the selection. Read the selection. Use the following steps for each recommended word to determine if it requires brief instruction or elaborate instruction. Teach no more than 10 words per selection.

1. Does the word belong in the misdirective or nondirective category? If so, proceed to Step 2. This word may be a candidate for the word bank. If not, proceed to the next word. Descriptions of the natural context categories are as follows:

   - Misdirective: The context leads the reader toward the incorrect meaning of the word.

   - Nondirective: The context does not assist the reader in determining the meaning of the target word.

   - Directive: There is enough information to lead the reader to the correct meaning of the word, or the word is explicitly defined or explained in the text.

   - General: The context provides the reader with adequate information to give a general idea of the word's meaning.

2. Is the word critical (i.e., conceptually central) for understanding the selection? If so, proceed to Step 3. If not, proceed to the next word.

3. Next, consider the student factors.

   a. Ask yourself if the students had sufficient previous experience with or exposure to the word.

   b. Ask yourself if the word will be important for students to know 5 years from now.

   c. Write the word in the word bank if you decided that students have not had sufficient previous experience with or exposure to the word and it will be important for them to know 5 years from now. Repeat Steps 1–3 for the remaining words before proceeding to Step 4.

CUMULATIVE REVIEW II

4. Determine whether each word in the word bank is a Tier 1, Tier 2, or Tier 3 word. Enter each word in the appropriate column. Descriptions of the tiers are as follows:

- Tier 1 are the most basic words (e.g., *desk, run, house*). Students rarely need to be taught these words.

- Tier 2 are high frequency words for mature language users and are found across a variety of subject areas (e.g., *adequate, enormous, vociferous, satisfactory*).

- Tier 3 words are used infrequently and are often limited to a specific subject area (e.g., *chlorophyll, archipelago, diode, ventricle*).

5. Circle the Tier 2 words that are most necessary for comprehending the selection. Again, consider such factors as the importance of the word for understanding the selection, students' knowledge of and exposure to the word, the importance for future learning, students' socioeconomic status (SES), and students' English language proficiency.

6. Circle the Tier 1 and Tier 3 words that are critical for comprehending the selection.

7. Decide which of the circled words need only brief instruction. Enter those words in the Brief Instruction column.

8. Decide which of the circled words need more elaborate instruction. Enter those words in the Elaborate Instruction column.

Selecting Words to Teach Table

Selection: _____

Word bank		

Tier 1	Tier 2	Tier 3

Brief instruction	Elaborate instruction

Note: Remember to teach no more than 10 words per selection.

Copyright © 2009 by Paul H. Brookes Publishing Co., Inc. All rights reserved.

9

**WORKSHEET
9C**

Task Analysis

*Student Friendly/Not Student
Friendly, Examples,
Nonexamples, Concrete
Representations, and Activities
to Promote Word Learning*

Directions: Use the following steps to determine whether the publisher's definitions for the words you entered in the Brief and Elaborate Instruction columns are student friendly or not student friendly and whether the instructional recommendations include examples, nonexamples, concrete representations, and activities to promote word learning.

1. Read the definition for the first recommended word.

2. Determine whether the definition is student friendly. Indicate your decision by writing the word in either the Student Friendly or Not Student Friendly column of Worksheet 9D: Student Friendly/Not Student Friendly, Examples, Nonexamples, Concrete Representations, Activity Table. Student friendly definitions contain two important elements:

   • Characterize the word: Student friendly definitions describe a word by focusing on specific aspects of its meaning rather than on a general description.

   • Explain meanings in everyday language: Definitions use words that are part of the student's vocabulary and convey the connotation of a word.

3. Now that you have decided whether the definition is student friendly, read the instructional recommendations for teaching the word. Determine whether these recommendations include examples within and beyond the context of the selection. Also, determine whether nonexamples, concrete representations, and activities that give students the opportunity to interact with words are included. If they are present, place a checkmark in the appropriate columns using Worksheet 9D: Student Friendly/Not Student Friendly, Examples, Nonexamples, Concrete Representations, Activity Table.

4. Repeat Steps 1–3 until you address all recommended words.

WORKSHEET 9D

Student Friendly/Not Student Friendly, Examples, Nonexamples, Concrete Representations, Activity Table

Selection: _____

Student friendly	Example within context	Nonexample	Example beyond context	Concrete representation

Selection: _____

Not student friendly	Example within context	Nonexample	Example beyond context	Concrete representation

WORKSHEET 9E

Examples of Activities to Promote Word Learning

(Source: Beck, McKeown, & Kucan, 2002)

Describing/Explaining

1. **Word Associations** requires students to associate a known word with a newly learned word to reinforce the meaning of the new word and to promote cumulative review. This helps students embed the newly learned words into their vocabulary. Examples of word associations include the following for the words *murmur, benevolent, fragrant,* and *vociferous*:

    a. Which word goes with *flowers*? Why?

    b. Which word goes with *whisper*? Why?

    c. Which word goes with *helping*? Why?

    d. Which word goes with *loud*? Why?

2. **"Have You Ever...?"** helps students associate newly learned words based on their background knowledge and experiences. Examples of this include the following:

    a. When might you *contradict* someone?

    b. When might you *waver* in your decision?

    c. When might you *criticize* something?

3. **Applause** directs students to indicate, by the volume of their clapping, how much they would like to be described by the words presented (i.e., not very much, a little, very much). Students are asked to explain why they would feel that way. Examples include the following:

    a. Alert

    b. Impudent

    c. Visible

    d. Headstrong

4. **Idea Completion** expects students to incorporate a word's meaning into a context to explain a situation. Examples of idea completion include the following:

   a.   The small child was *forbidden* to play with the matches because...

   b.   Right before Sarah made her debut in the dance recital, she *scanned* the audience to...

   Variations of Idea Completion examples include the following:

   a.   Would you want a *frail* person on your football team? Why? Why not?

   b.   What might cause an entire classroom of math students to be *baffled*?

   c.   When might you need a *navigator*?

   d.   When might you *cease* your activity?

   e.   Why might you *wince*?

   f.   What would make you feel *timid*? Why?

   g.   Do you ever feel *alert*? When? Why?

   h.   Have you ever been *persistent*? What happened?

5. **Questions, Reasons, and Examples** provides opportunities for students to interact with target words by responding to questions and giving examples. Examples include the following:

   a.   Why is it good to *contemplate* the possible consequences of your behavior?

   b.   What could you say to *convince* your parents to let you have a dog?

   c.   What is something you would *boycott* in protest of low wages for farm workers?

   d.   Which of the following might be *appetizing*? Why?

   The scent of flowers or the smell of chocolate?

   The smell of freshly baked cookies or grass that has just been cut?

   The smell of pizza or burning wood?

6. **Multiple Meanings** gives students practice in applying various meanings to the same word. Examples include the following:

   a.   Word: *litter*

   What does the word *litter* mean to a veterinarian, a custodian, and a medic?

   b.   Word: *scent*

   What does the word *scent* mean to a chef and a bloodhound?

   c.   Word: *crescent*

   What does the word *crescent* mean to a baker, an astronomer, and a mapmaker?

Examples/Nonexamples

1. **Making Choices** encourages students to make choices and justify responses about a word's meaning. Examples include the following:

   a. If any of the following might make someone experience *dread*, say, "dread." Be ready to explain your answer.

   Getting a new puppy

   Hearing a strange noise

   Taking a big test

   Writing a thank you note

   Looking over the edge of a canyon

   b. I'll say some things. If they sound *impudent*, say, "impudent." If they sound *courteous*, say "courteous." Be ready to explain your answer.

   No, thank you.

   That's not the way you pronounce it!

   My mom can cook better than you can.

   May I have some more?

   You didn't give me as much as you gave her!

   c. If any of the things I say might be examples of *philanthropy* say, "philanthropy." If not, don't say anything. Be ready to explain your answer.

   Helping to feed the children of Somalia

   Giving money to your children to help them buy a house

   Helping with a fundraiser to fight breast cancer

   Donating money to a school club in exchange for advertising your company's business

   Donating money to help eradicate malaria and river blindness

   d. If a dog is *timid*, would you pet it or leave it alone? Why?

   e. Is *forage* something your brother would do or something your rabbit would do? Why?

   f. If you had a *sufficient* number of cards, would your deck be complete? Why? Why not?

   g. What would make you feel *indignant*, being chosen for the neighborhood baseball team or being left off of the invitation list for a birthday party? Why?

2. **Child-Created Examples** requires students to create examples that demonstrate their thinking about how the word relates to their background knowledge and life experiences. Examples include the following:

   a. If your parents set up *consequences* for your poor behavior, what might they be?

   b. If your sister persisted in *embarrassing* you in front of your friends, how would you respond?

3. **Facets of Word Meaning** stimulates a discussion among students about the critical features of a word's meaning. In this activity, students choose and justify the example that illustrates a word's connotation. Examples include the following:

   a. Word: *persist*

   During a car trip, a child asks every mile, "Are we there yet?"

   At a rest stop, a child asks for a soda.

   b. Word: *verify*

   You need to complete any assignments missed during absences.

   You need to bring a note from your parents when you are absent.

   c. Word: *commitment*

   The skater continued with her lessons, practicing five days a week for several hours each day, until the time of the competition.

   Sam practices his trumpet every chance he gets, but his schedule is quite hectic so he rarely gets to it every day.

   d. Word: *vicariously*

   The mother felt as if she, rather than her daughter, was having an operation to repair her broken arm.

   The mother sat in the operating room worried as she awaited the results of her daughter's surgery.

Relationships Among Words

Using All of the Words

It is important to develop practice items that include all target words from the selection being read. In the following activity under the subtopic Sentences, all of the words can be incorporated into one practice item or sentence; however, often it is difficult to find a relationship among all of the target words that can fit easily into one thought or idea. The activities titled Choices and One Context for All of the Words illustrate how to develop practice items in cases where all of the target words cannot easily be incorporated into one sentence.

1. **Relating Words** encourages students to explain and justify their responses to questions and choose words that fit the descriptions given in the sentence. Examples include the following:

   a.   Using two words

   Would you *dread* something *appetizing*? Why? Why not?

   When does the moon *cease* being *visible*?

   When might you *verify* a *presumption*?

   If you were in *excruciating* pain, would you *wince*? Why? Why not?

   b.   Sentences

   Target words from the selection: *waver, contemplating, sufficient, sacrifice, cease*

   Would you *waver* while *contemplating* sharing cookies with your brother if you thought there was not a *sufficient* number, or would you *sacrifice* some cookies to *cease* arguing? Why?

   c.   Choices

   Target words from the selection: *timid, compliant, persistent, frail*

   If you do not want to go to a beach party because there are too many new people to meet, are you *frail* or *timid*? Why?

   If a child refuses to put away his things every time his mother asks him, is he *persistent* or *compliant*? Why?

2. **One Context for All of the Words** promotes students' thinking about the relationship among target words in a selection by asking questions that require knowledge of the words. In the following examples, the words *procrastinate, ramifications,* and *justify* are used in the context of situations involving homework.

   a.   Why would you *procrastinate* doing your homework?

   b.   What would be the *ramifications* of not doing your homework?

   c.   How would you *justify* not completing your homework?

Assessment

Assessments are used to measure students' knowledge of words. The most common format is multiple choice. The previously described activities that promote multiple meaningful exposures can also be used as a valid way to assess a student's acquisition of vocabulary. Following are a few more examples:

1. **Describing/Explaining**

    a. Describe how someone behaves that shows he or she is *indignant*.

    b. Tell about a time you were *baffled*.

    c. Explain a situation that might make someone *wince*.

    d. Mom was excited when she realized that not only was her son accepted by one of the most *prestigious* universities in the country, but he had also been given a full scholarship for the entire time he will be attending. Explain why Mom was so *elated*.

    e. Place the following phrases on the word line from Little Endurance to Great Deal of Endurance and explain your placement. How much endurance does it take to . . .

        be a spectator at a *decathlon*?

        undergo an *appendectomy*?

        tolerate a child who is having a *tantrum*?

        listen to a *tedious* speaker for over an hour?

        Little Endurance .... Great Deal of Endurance

    f. Place the following phrases on the word line from A Little Anxious to Very Anxious and explain your placement. How anxious would you be if . . .

        you were waiting to see if you received the *position* you wanted?

        airport officials just announced that the mechanical *malfunction* was repaired and the flight would be leaving as scheduled?

        the results of the contest were just about to be *conveyed* to the participants?

        your passport was *invalid*?

        A Little Anxious .... Very Anxious

2. **Relationships Among Words**

    What is alike and/or different between these pairs of words? Explain.

    headstrong/persistent

    timid/frail

    dread/dismay

    waver/baffled

3. **Examples/Nonexamples**

Beat the Clock: Give students 90 seconds to complete 14 items. This activity assesses the students' ability to quickly access words' meanings.

a.	*Timid* mice stay out of sight.	True	False
b.	*Impudent* children are welcome everywhere.	True	False
c.	*Persistent* people give up easily.	True	False
d.	Success is a *consequence* of hard work.	True	False
e.	It is impolite to *stare* at people.	True	False
f.	A restaurant has *sufficient* food.	True	False
g.	The moon is never shaped like a *crescent*.	True	False
h.	The black piano keys were *ebony*.	True	False
i.	The garden is *fragrant* in winter.	True	False
j.	The teacher was *indignant* at my *impudence*.	True	False
k.	Edison *persisted* until he created a light bulb.	True	False
l.	The players *disperse* during Hide and Seek.	True	False
m.	The teacher *presumes* we will fail our test.	True	False
n.	Grandpa was *frail* while recovering from surgery.	True	False

REFERENCE

Beck, I.L., McKeown, M.G., & Kucan, L. (2002). *Bringing words to life: Robust vocabulary instruction.* New York: Guilford Press.

Vocabulary Lesson
Design Framework

Target word:

Student friendly definition:

Concrete representation:

Examples within context of selection:
(Note: Remember to tell students why these are examples of the target word.)

Concrete representation:

Examples beyond context of selection:
(Note: Remember to tell students why these are examples of the target word.)

Concrete representation:

Nonexamples:
(Note: Remember to tell students why these are not examples of the target word.)

Concrete representation:

Learning How to Improve Vocabulary Instruction Through Teacher Study Groups by Joseph Dimino & Mary Jo Taylor   177
Copyright © 2009 by Paul H. Brookes Publishing Co., Inc. All rights reserved.

CUMULATIVE REVIEW II

Activity 1 to promote word learning

Activity 2 to promote word learning

Learning How to Improve Vocabulary Instruction Through Teacher Study Groups by Joseph Dimino & Mary Jo Taylor
Copyright © 2009 by Paul H. Brookes Publishing Co., Inc. All rights reserved.

Task Analysis

Selecting Words to Teach (Teacher-Selected Words)

Directions: If fewer than five words were targeted for brief and elaborate instruction, choose additional words from the selection. Use the following steps for each additional word to determine if it requires brief or elaborate instruction. Teach no more than 10 words per selection.

1. Does the word belong in the misdirective or nondirective category? If so, proceed to Step 2. This word may be a candidate for the word bank. If not, proceed to the next word. Descriptions of the natural context categories are as follows:

   • Misdirective: The context leads the reader toward the incorrect meaning of the word.

   • Nondirective: The context does not assist the reader in determining the meaning of the target word.

   • Directive: There is enough information to lead the reader to the correct meaning of the word, or the word is explicitly defined or explained in the text.

   • General: The context provides the reader with adequate information to give a general idea of the word's meaning.

2. Is the word critical (i.e., conceptually central) for understanding the selection? If so, proceed to Step 3. If not, proceed to the next word.

3. Next, consider the students factors.

   a. Ask yourself if the students have had sufficient previous experience with or exposure to the word.

   b. Ask yourself if the word will be important for students to know 5 years from now.

   c. Write the word in the word bank if you decided that students have not had sufficient previous experience with or exposure to the word and it will be important for students to know 5 years from now. Repeat Steps 1–3 for the remaining words before proceeding to Step 4.

4. Determine whether each word in the word bank is a Tier 1, Tier 2, or Tier 3 word. Enter each word in the appropriate column. Descriptions of the tiers are as follows:

   - Tier 1 are the most basic words (e.g., *desk, run, house*). Students rarely need to be taught these words.

   - Tier 2 are high frequency words for mature language users and are found across a variety of subject areas (e.g., *adequate, enormous, vociferous, satisfactory*).

   - Tier 3 words are used infrequently and are often limited to a specific subject area (e.g., *chlorophyll, archipelago, diode, ventricle*).

5. Circle the Tier 2 words that are most necessary for comprehending the selection. Again, consider factors such as the importance of the word for understanding the selection, students' knowledge of and exposure to the word, the importance for future learning, socioeconomic status (SES), and English language proficiency.

6. Circle the Tier 1 and Tier 3 words that are critical for comprehending the selection.

7. Decide which of the circled words need only brief instruction. Enter those words in the Brief Instruction column.

8. Decide which of the circled words need more elaborate instruction. Enter those words in the Elaborate Instruction column.

Answer Key

THIS APPENDIX CONTAINS ANSWERS FOR THE FOLLOWING WORKSHEETS:

- Worksheet 1C: Study Guide: Words in Context
- Worksheet 2B: Study Guide: Selecting Words to Teach
- Worksheet 2C: Semantic Map: Selecting Words to Teach
- Worksheet 3B: Study Guide: Student Friendly Definitions
- Worksheet 3C: Activity: Student Friendly Definitions, First Grade
- Worksheet 3C: Activity: Student Friendly Definitions, Second Grade
- Worksheet 3C: Activity: Student Friendly Definitions, Third Grade
- Worksheet 3C: Activity: Student Friendly Definitions, Fourth Grade
- Worksheet 3C: Activity: Student Friendly Definitions, Fifth Grade
- Worksheet 3C: Activity: Student Friendly Definitions, Sixth Grade
- Worksheet 4B: Study Guide: Examples, Nonexamples, and Concrete Representations
- Worksheet 4C: Instructional Framework Table
- Worksheet 5B: Study Guide: Activities to Promote Word Learning
- Worksheet 7B: Study Guide: Using Context to Determine Word Meanings

**ANSWER KEY
WORKSHEET
1C**

Study Guide

Words in Context

Directions: Determine the context category (i.e., misdirective, nondirective, directive, or general) of the bolded words in each of the following paragraphs.

1. When they visited the desert retreat, Judy and her mother enjoyed swimming, playing tennis, and having spa treatments in the cactus gardens. Because of the effects of the **sere** weather, they had moisturizing facials every day. Even so, they were happy to return to their beachfront home.

    Context Category: _____General_____

    Definition: Arid or dry

    In this passage, the meaning of **sere** is not explicitly stated. However, the information conveys the idea that sere has something to do with arid or dry weather:

    a. They were at a desert retreat where the spa treatments are in the cactus garden (typically deserts are dry, hot, and grow cacti).

    b. They had moisturizing facials every day (the arid desert climate dries out the skin).

    c. They were happy to return to their beachfront home (the weather conditions at the beach are the opposite of the desert).

    d. *Sere* is used as an adjective to describe the weather conditions.

2. We were having our annual staff luncheon at the local Italian restaurant, Giuseppe's Trattoria. The food was excellent and our large group was having a wonderful time. Gaetano, the owner, was **equanimous** when several of his relatives dropped in unexpectedly.

    Context Category: _____Nondirective_____

    Definition: A person who is even tempered, especially in a difficult or stressful situation

    It is not possible to determine the meaning of **equanimous**. In the context of this passage it could mean delighted, upset, happy, depressed, and so forth. The context does not provide clues that would enable readers to use their background knowledge to derive a general meaning of the word.

3. There are many similarities and differences between mammals and birds. The bone structure of a bird's wing bears an uncanny resemblance to the bone structure of the human arm. The **hallux**, or big toe, of most mammals aligns with the other toes. In birds, the comparable digit usually turns backward.

Context Category: _____Directive_____

The word is defined in the context.

4. A group of residents had gathered in the coffeehouse to visit and listen to the weekly literary readings and interpretations by a local college professor known for his eloquent speaking style. The audience was impressed by the speaker's use of **vernacular** language when reading his newest poetry.

Context Category: _____Misdirective_____

Definition: The language or dialect that is most widely spoken by ordinary people in a region or country. (Macaulay & Seaton, 2003, p. 1618)

Readers might assume that **vernacular** means the literary or flowery language that is stereotypically attributed to poets. The author indicates that a professor, with the reputation of having an eloquent speaking style, is going to read and interpret poetry. This description would lead the reader to the incorrect meaning.

ANSWER KEY
WORKSHEET
2B

Study Guide

Selecting Words to Teach

1. Choose a statement from Worksheet 2A: Selecting Words to Teach that you think is important and explain why.

   Answers may vary.

2. Sort the following words into tiers.

justify	rain	key
solstice	intrigue	star
diode	aorta	extraordinary

Tier 1	Tier 2	Tier 3
rain	justify	solstice
key	extraordinary	diode
star	intrigue	aorta

Semantic Map

Selecting Words to Teach

Importance

1. Conceptually central: Needed to know to comprehend the key concepts in the selection
2. Important: Needed for understanding the gist but not central to the selection
3. Useful: Not crucial for understanding the selection
4. Unimportant: Unnecessary for understanding the selection

Usefulness

1. Tier 1: Most basic words
2. Tier 2: High frequency words that are found across a variety of subject areas for mature language learners
3. Tier 3: Words that are used infrequently and often limited to a specific subject area

Selecting Words to Teach

Student Factors

1. Consider the students' grade placement.
2. Ask if the students had previous experience with or exposure to the word.
3. Ask if the word will be important for students to know 5 years from now.

Natural Context

1. Misdirective: The context leads the reader toward the incorrect meaning of the word.
2. Nondirective: The context does not assist the reader in determining the meaning of the target word.
3. Directive: There is enough information to lead the reader to the correct meaning of the word or the word is explicitly defined or explained in the text.
4. General: The context provides the reader with adequate information to give him or her a general idea of the word's meaning.

Study Guide

Student Friendly Definitions

1. List two reasons why teachers should use student friendly definitions when teaching vocabulary.

   Most definitions do not adequately convey meanings that students can understand. Students mistakenly interpret one or two words from dictionary definitions as the word's entire meaning.

2. What should a good dictionary definition convey?

   A good dictionary definition should convey the word's connotation (i.e., how the word is typically used) and an explanation that students are able to understand.

Double Journal Entry

Directions: On the right side of the following double entry journal, write your reactions to the statements taken from Worksheet 3A: Student Friendly Definitions.

Responses to the statements will vary.

Statements	Reactions
1. Educators should use effective vehicles that result in "deep and sustained knowledge of words" (Beck, McKeown, & Kucan, 2002, p. 32).	
2. Using dictionary definitions sometimes gets in the way of understanding word meanings, especially to a naive learner who has little or no knowledge of the word.	

Activity

Student Friendly Definitions

First Grade

Directions: Determine whether the definitions for the words below are student friendly. Indicate your decision by circling Friendly or Unfriendly.

1. *Precious*: of great value or high price

   Friendly   **Unfriendly**

   A student friendly definition would be the following: If you say that something, such as a resource, is precious, you mean that it is valuable and should not be wasted or used badly.

2. *Wonderful*: exciting

   Friendly   **Unfriendly**

   A student friendly definition would be the following: If you describe someone or something as wonderful, you think the person or the thing is extremely good.

3. *Amazing*: You say something is amazing when it is very surprising and makes you feel pleasure, approval, or wonder.

   Friendly   Unfriendly

Activity

Student Friendly Definitions

Second Grade

Directions: Determine whether the definitions for the words below are student friendly. Indicate your decision by circling Friendly or Unfriendly.

1. *Hungry*: When you are hungry you want food because you have not eaten for some time and have an uncomfortable or painful feeling in your stomach.

    Friendly   Unfriendly

2. *Protect*: to cover or shield from exposure, injury, damage, or destruction

    Friendly   **Unfriendly**

    A student friendly definition would be the following: To protect someone or something means to prevent them from being harmed or damaged.

3. *Statue*: a large sculpture modeled or carved out of a material such as stone, clay, metal, or wood

    Friendly   Unfriendly

Activity

Student Friendly Definitions

Third Grade

Directions: Determine whether the definitions for the words below are student friendly. Indicate your decision by circling Friendly or Unfriendly.

1. *Sensible*: of a kind to be felt or perceived: as a: perceptible to the senses or to reason or understanding

    Friendly   **Unfriendly**

    A student friendly definition would be the following: Sensible actions or decisions are good because they are based on reasons rather than emotions.

2. *Splendid*: If you say something is splendid, you mean it is very good.

    Friendly   Unfriendly

3. *Brave*: having or showing courage

    Friendly   **Unfriendly**

    A student friendly definition would be the following: Someone who is brave is willing to do things that are dangerous and does not show fear in difficult or dangerous situations.

Activity

Student Friendly Definitions

Fourth Grade

Directions: Determine whether the definitions for the words below are student friendly. Indicate your decision by circling Friendly or Unfriendly.

1. *Crime*: an act or the commission of an act that is forbidden or the omission of a duty that is commanded by a public law and that makes the offender liable to punishment by that law

    Friendly   **Unfriendly**

    A student friendly definition would be the following: A crime is an illegal action or activity for which a person can be punished by the law.

2. *Outspoken*: direct and open in speech or expression

    Friendly   **Unfriendly**

    A student friendly definition would be the following: People who are outspoken give their opinions about things openly and honestly, even if they are likely to shock or offend people.

3. *Taunt*: what someone does if they say unkind or insulting things to you, especially about your weaknesses or failures

    Friendly   Unfriendly

Activity

Student Friendly Definitions

Fifth Grade

Directions: Determine whether the definitions for the words below are student friendly. Indicate your decision by circling Friendly or Unfriendly.

1. *Oppose*: to place over against something so as to provide resistance, counterbalance, or contrast

    Friendly   **Unfriendly**

    A student friendly definition would be the following: If you oppose someone, their plans, or their ideas, you disagree with what they want to do and try to prevent them from doing it.

2. *Disappointed*: sad because something has not happened or because something is not as good as you had hoped

    Friendly   Unfriendly

3. *Dread*: to fear greatly

    Friendly   **Unfriendly**

    A student friendly definition would be the following: If you dread something that may happen, you feel very nervous, worried, and unhappy about it because you think it will be unpleasant or upsetting.

Activity

Student Friendly Definitions

Sixth Grade

Directions: Determine whether the definitions for the words below are student friendly. Indicate your decision by circling Friendly or Unfriendly.

1. *Hoax*: a trick in which someone tells people a lie (e.g., saying there is a bomb somewhere when there is not, saying that a painting is a genuine when it is not)

    Friendly   Unfriendly

2. *Conserve*: to keep in a safe or sound state

    Friendly   **Unfriendly**

    A student friendly definition would be the following: If you conserve a supply of something, you use it carefully so that it lasts for a long time.

3. *Amiable*: someone who is friendly and pleasant

    Friendly   Unfriendly

Study Guide

Examples, Nonexamples, and Concrete Representations

1. Why is it important to provide examples within the context of a selection?

    Providing examples beyond the context of the selection helps to clarify and pinpoint a word's meaning.

2. Why is it important to provide examples beyond the context of the story?

    a. It assists students in formulating a logical, unambiguous understanding of a word.

    b. It helps students who may be inclined to limit a word's connotation to the circumstances the teacher described when introducing the word.

3. Explain why providing contrasting examples is a critical feature of strong vocabulary instruction.

    Contrasting or nonexamples help solidify meanings and prevent misconceptions by explicitly telling students the attributes that are not part of a word's connotation.

4. What is the advantage of using concrete representations of a word?

    It allows students to make a connection between language—something abstract—and something tangible. Language is being translated into a real image.

Double Entry Journal

Directions: On the right side of the following Double Entry Journal, write your reactions to the statements taken from the Worksheet 4A: Examples, Nonexamples, and Concrete Representations regarding examples and nonexamples.

Answers may vary.

Statements	Reactions
1. Examples beyond the context of the selection help students who may be inclined to limit the word's connotation to the circumstances the teacher described when introducing the word.	
2. Contrasting, discriminating examples help pinpoint the meaning of the word by providing instances in which the definition does not apply.	

Instructional Framework Table

Directions: Match the set of statements describing the instructional sequence with the phases and examples.

1. Students are given an example beyond the context of the selection with a concrete representation.

2. Students complete activities without teacher guidance.

3. Students are given an example within the context of the selection with a concrete representation.

4. The meaning of a word is explained in student friendly terms with a concrete representation.

5. The teacher leads an activity to check students' understanding of a word's meaning.

6. The teacher taps students' prior knowledge.

7. The teacher provides a nonexample.

Instructional Framework Table

Target word: ___enormous___

Phase of instruction	Sequence of instruction	Example
Activating background	6. The teacher taps into and/or develops prior knowledge.	Teacher (T): Can anyone think of a time when you saw something that was really big?
Explaining/modeling	4. The meaning of the word is explained in student friendly terms with a concrete representation.	T: Something that is *enormous* is very big in size or amount. (Teacher makes a gesture with her arms.)
Explaining/modeling	3. Students are given an example within the context of the selection with a concrete representation.	T: In this story, Sydney has an exciting adventure when he takes a vacation to see the *enormous* redwood trees. He describes them as *enormous* because they are so huge. Many of them are more than 200 feet high. (Teacher shows a picture of a redwood tree.)

Phase of instruction	Sequence of instruction	Example
Explaining/modeling	1. Students are given an example beyond the context of the selection with a concrete representation.	T: We also use the word *enormous* when we describe a large amount of something. When we took a tour of the recycling center, we saw *enormous* amounts of old newspapers. This was an *enormous* amount because there were hundreds of stacks of newspapers. (The teacher shows a photograph she took of these stacks.)
Explaining/modeling	7. The teacher provides a nonexample.	T: The maple trees on our school grounds are not *enormous* compared with a redwood. Mice and ants would not be described as *enormous* because they are small.
Guided practice	5. The teacher leads an activity to check students' understanding of the word's meaning.	The teacher conducts this activity with the class: T: If any of these things I say are examples of something *enormous*, say, "*enormous*." 1. A dinosaur 2. A laptop computer 3. A mansion
Independent practice	2. Students complete activities without teacher guidance.	After the lesson is taught, students are asked to complete this writing exercise as homework. Would something *enormous* fit in your pocket? Why? Why not? Would something *enormous* fit in the ocean? Why? Why not? Would something *enormous* fit in a football field? Why? Why not?

**ANSWER KEY
WORKSHEET
5B**

Study Guide

Activities to Promote Word Learning

1. Describe the three levels of processing categorized by Stahl (1999).

   Association: This is the lowest level of difficulty. This level of cognitive processing uses rote memorization of definitions and activities that require simple matching or association (e.g., crossword puzzles, matching exercises, Hangman).

   Comprehension: This cognitive processing requires students to classify words, determine relationships among words, give examples and nonexamples, and describe attributes of the words.

   Generative: This level of cognitive processing involves thinking at the highest level of difficulty of word learning. Students are required to use information to develop or construct meaning and give unique and inventive responses to questions about words.

2. What is the advantage of using activities that require students to use generative processing over those that only require processing at the association or comprehension levels?

   Word learning at the generative processing level requires students to construct unique and inventive responses that include a justification of their responses. It promotes learning words at a conceptual level, limiting the possibility that students will develop misunderstandings or only vague understandings of words' meanings.

Study Guide

Using Context to Determine Word Meanings

Directions: Read each paragraph and determine the meaning of the italicized target word by using the following steps of the word learning strategy. Write your definition in the space provided. Indicate which sentence(s) contain the clues that helped you develop your definition (e.g., the sentence containing the target word; the sentence before, and the sentence after).

1. Read the sentence with the target word, and look for clues to help you figure out the meaning of the word.

2. Read the sentences before and after the sentence with the target word. Look for clues to help you figure out the meaning of the word.

3. When you think you know what the word means, substitute your meaning for the target word in the sentence. If it makes sense, continue reading. If it doesn't make sense, try the strategy again.

Our friend, the famous wildlife artist, had a rather intense interest in wolves, dogs, foxes, and similar four-legged beasts. His studio always had at least a few residents, sometimes a Chihuahua, at other times a rather wolfish-looking shepherd mix. We were always a little nervous around the *canid* skulls on his window ledge. It would be impolite to ask him whether they were fossils for artistic inspiration or mementos of his past companions.

> Definition: <u>any of a family (canidae) of carnivorous animals that includes wolves,</u>
> <u>jackals, foxes, and the domestic dog (Merriam-Webster Online Dictionary, 2009)</u>
>
> In which sentence(s) did you find the clues? <u>The clues were found in the sentence</u>
> <u>after the one containing the target word.</u>
>
> Explain how the clues helped you figure out the definition. <u>The sentence **after** indi-</u>
> <u>cates that the author wondered whether the skulls on the window ledge were those of</u>
> <u>companions (i.e., pets) the artist had in the past. Because the artist always has dogs</u>
> <u>as pets, *canid* skulls could mean dog skulls.</u>
>
> When you think you know what the word means, substitute your meaning for the target word in the sentence. If it makes sense, continue reading. If it doesn't make sense, try the strategy again. "We were always a little nervous around the *dog* skulls on his window ledge."

Sarah was having more and more difficulty staying awake through the seemingly endless lectures in the science hall. Finally, when she could not read her notes for the upcoming final exam, she went into her study and made the call. Later that evening, she approached her husband with the news: "Clarence, I have made an appointment for you with a doctor who specializes in *somniloquy*. I want you to go because the sounds you are making when you sleep keep me awake at night and it is affecting my grades."

Definition: <u>the act or habit of talking in one's sleep (Pickett, 2000)</u>

In which sentence(s) did you find the clues? <u>The clues were found in the sentence after</u>
<u>the one containing the target word.</u>

Explain how the clues helped you figure out the definition. <u>The sentence **after** the tar-</u>
<u>get word indicates why Sarah cannot stay awake in class and sheds light on the defini-</u>
<u>tion of *somniloquy*. She cannot sleep because her husband is making sounds in his</u>
<u>sleep. To rectify the situation, they are going to a doctor who specializes in *somnilo-*</u>
<u>*quy*. Therefore *somniloquy* refers to some type of a sleep disorder.</u>

When you think you know what the word means, substitute your meaning for the target word in the sentence. If it makes sense, continue reading. If it doesn't make sense,
try the strategy again. "Later that evening, she approached her husband with the
news: 'Clarence, I have made an appointment for you with a doctor who specializes in
sleep disorders.'"

Tabloid papers available at every supermarket checkout line scream insane headlines:
"Civil War Baby Found at Battlefield," "Ninety-year-old Woman Pregnant with Triplets!"
Editors must think that the people who read their publication are unaware, oblivious, unintelligent, and uninformed, sharing a common assertion that individuals who read tabloids
are *nescient* readers. I can only hope people who buy these publications at least try to verify some of the printed information.

Definition: <u>lack of knowledge or awareness: ignorance (Merriam-Webster Online</u>
<u>Dictionary, 2009)</u>

In which sentence(s) did you find the clues? <u>The clues are in the same sentence as the</u>
<u>target word.</u>

Explain how the clues helped you figure out the definition. <u>The sentence containing</u>
<u>the target word contains many clues to help the reader determine its meaning. At the</u>
<u>beginning of the sentence, the author states that editors must think people who read</u>
<u>tabloids are unaware, oblivious, unintelligent, and uninformed. As the sentence con-</u>
<u>tinues, the meaning of the target word becomes clearer. The author connects those at-</u>
<u>tributes by inferring that they may be synonyms for the target word, *nescient*.</u>

When you think you know what the word means, substitute your meaning for the target word in the sentence. If it makes sense, continue reading. If it doesn't make sense,
try the strategy again. "Editors must think that the people who read their publication
are unaware, oblivious, unintelligent, and uninformed, sharing a common assertion
that individuals who read tabloids are _____ readers." The adjectives *unaware,*
oblivious, unintelligent, and *uninformed* make sense in the sentence.

REFERENCES

canid. (2009). In *Merriam-Webster online dictionary*. Retrieved January 20, 2009, from
    http://www.merriam-webster.com/dictionary/canid
nescient. (2009). In *Merriam-Webster online dictionary*. Retrieved January 20, 2009, from
    http://www.merriam-webster.com/dictionary/nescient
Pickett, J.P. (Ed.). (2000). *The American heritage dictionary of the English language* (4th
    ed.). Boston: Houghton Mifflin Company.